A MONOGRAPHIC STUDY

ANI STOYKOVA

MARIYA PASKALEVA

SOUTHEAST EUROPEAN CAPITAL MARKETS: DYNAMICS, RELATIONSHIP AND SOVEREIGN CREDIT RISK

ISBN: 978-3-11-064831-7

Contents

Introduction 3

CHAPTER ONE: Integration of Southeast European Capital Markets 6

1.1. Studies on the integration of Southeast European Capital Markets 6

1.2. Research Methodology 9

1.3. Research Data 14

1.4. Empirical results for the integration of Southeast European Capital Markets 16

CHAPTER TWO: Impact of sentiment indicators on the capital market dynamics and default probability 27

2.1. Studies on the impact of sentiment indicators on the capital market dynamics and default probability 27

2.2. Research Methodology 29

2.3. Data research 31

2.4. Empirical results for the impact of sentiment indicators on the capital market dynamics and default probability 32

CHAPTER THREE: Sovereign CDS Spread determinants and their impact on the competitiveness of the Bulgarian economy 42

3.1. Studies on sovereign CDS Spread determinants and their impact on the competitiveness of the economy 42

3.2. Research methodology, Hypothesis and Data 44

3.3. Research results and Discussion 48

CHAPTER FOUR: Relationship between Bulgarian sovereign credit risk and accounting information . 55

4.1. Studies on the relationship between Bulgarian sovereign credit risk and accounting information 55

4.2. Reaserch Methodology and data 56

4.3. Research results and Discussion 62

Conclusion 69

REFERENCES 74

Appendixes 83

Introduction

Over the last 30 years, financial markets have become more integrated mainly because of reducing value of information, the development of electronic trading systems and the removal of the legal restrictions on international capital flows. These changes lead to a stronger interaction between the international financial markets and also expend the capital movements. What is more, according to the portfolio theory, profits from the international diversification of the financial instruments portfolio are inversely related to the correlation of returns of these financial instruments. In the context of this theory investors are becoming more active by investing in the foreign capital markets as a part of the risk diversification strategy. The tendency for the global markets to become integrated and harmonized is a result of the increasing tendency toward liberalization and deregulation in the money and capital markets, both in developed and developing countries. Such liberalization is important to introduce structural reforms, to promote market efficiency, to estimate investment, and to create a necessary climate for promoting sustainable economic growth. As a result, in the contest of portfolio theory there is an increase in correlations between financial markets leading to reduce the benefits of international diversification. The analysis of the capital markets integration represents an important topic in financial area as it possesses essential practical implications for assets allocation and investment management.

Capital markets in different countries or regions may show a diversified degree of integration, harmonization and segmentation. Rational investors should arbitrage between prices of the stock assets which actually resulting in more integrated markets. Since the last financial crisis, European countries have faced various challenges: consolidating their budgets while at the same time promoting economic growth and a collapse in gross domestic product (Stoilova, 2017). Further financial development and integration can help to improve the effectiveness of and the political incentives for structural reform. The consumer sentiment information and business sentiment information may influence on the capital market dynamics of therefore on the prices of financial assets. Additionally, the investors' expectations should be tested if they have predicting ability for capital markets' dynamic and the default probability.

As Ganchev (2015) emphasizes the last global financial crisis of 2007- 2008 is considered by many economists as the worst economic turmoil since the Great Depression. Over the last few years the development of Southeast European capital markets (SEE) has attracted more local investors, especially after the financial crisis. The occurrence of the global financial crisis and its reflection on European financial markets' stability has put credit default swaps (CDS) into a focus of attention. After the beginning of global financial and economic crisis, many economists have begun to consider credit default swap as one of the main indicator of sovereign country risk. Sovereign credit default swap spreads may be accepted as credit risk indicators that depend on investors' expectations. In addition, the countries in the same geographic region and also with the same group of investors are likely to have correlated capital markets. Consequently, the issue of the co-movement of the SEE capital markets, the investors' expectations are important for the local investors and companies in the region that are making capital budgeting decisions. In this study the joint movement of the SEE capital markets is examined although there are significant differences between SEE stock markets' characteristics. *Important contribution of this book is testing the investors' influence and accounting information on the Bulgarian capital markets and their relations with credit default swap spreads.*

In this study we find enough evidence that SEE capital markets are correlated and integrated and therefore these markets are characterized with harmonized and homogeneous market dynamics. The degree of the development of the SEE capital markets determines the linkages between them, while the reference capital markets are with weaker correlation in the group than the developing markets. The results reveal that there is a weak or moderate positive correlation between the reference capital markets of Turkey, Greece and Croatia and the other examined markets. The results show that strength of co-movement between Bulgarian stock market and the rest markets in Southeast Europe (SEE) is strong, especially with Serbian, Romanian and Croatian markets. The developing capital markets of the explored SEE group are determined mainly by their country- specific risk. The main contribution of this paper is that it provides further evidence on stock market integration and correlations in several SEE developing capital markets and three reference capital ones, emphasizing new linkages between Greek, Croatian, Turkish capital markets and the developing SEE stock ones. All things considered, it seems reasonable to assume that there is a strong correlation between SEE capital markets.

Bulgarian capital market is a part of the SEE group countries and it is a developing country and in the process of its development, people and investors should learn more about risk, credit risk management, and their relation to the rules of the listed companies and agencies. Many factors may provoke a change in stock prices: financial and monetary policies, macroeconomic conditions, investors' expectations and country's sovereign credit risk. According to Wang, Fu & Luo (2013) enterprise stock price is a comprehensive reflection of the company's future profit. Accepting sovereign CDS spreads as measurements of investment expectations regarding the development of Bulgarian capital market, we review the role of accounting information in CDS pricing because the accounting data may help investors make the most effective decision. The aim will be accomplished by creating an empirical model, based on the theoretical ones, including a panel data approach, several accounting variables, which are expected to have an impact on CDS spreads.

In this research, we analyze the joint movement of eleven financial markets of South East Europe (SEE) - Bulgaria, Croatia, Greece, Serbia, Slovenia, Turkey, Romania, Montenegro, Macedonia, Banja Luka and Sarajevo (Bosnia and Herzegovina) using correlation and regression analysis during the period 2005-2015. We reveal the role of investors' expectations on the capital markets dynamics and sovereign credit risk in Bulgaria.

Methodological and theoretical basis of the research can be formulated in the following sequence:

1. Theoretical analysis based on previous theoretical and empirical researches;
2. Development and implementation of practical econometric models. The analysis which reflects the quantitative results of the application of econometric methodology is based on the correlation analysis, VAR and GARCH models. *This is one of the main contributions of this research- the combination of linear and non- linear approaches in order to prove the research hypothesis;*

Restrictive conditions of this research are determined in the following aspects:

1. *Time range*-this research is restricted in the time interval from 2005- 2016;
2. *Methodological restrictions* –they are set by the statistical properties of the researched data imposing the application of specific econometric tests and models giving opportunity for the reflection. The proposed and used methodology does not claim to be the only possible and applicable when inspecting and proving the research thesis of this study.

3. *Place restrictions* – the analysis and the inspection of the research thesis are concentrated on Southeast European Capital Markets

4. Due to the aforementioned facts, conclusions drawn of this research do not engage processes and circumstances of other markets of the category of Southeast European Capital Markets

CHAPTER ONE: Integration of Southeast European Capital Markets

1.1. Studies on the integration of Southeast European Capital Markets

Many studies analyze the stock market co-movements among developed countries (Longin and Solnik, 1995; Forbes and Rigobon, 2002; Johnson and Soenen, 2003). Also, there are numerous studies concerning Central and Eastern Europe stock market co-movements (Kasch-Haroutounian and Price, 2001; Voronkova, 2004; Cappieollo, et al., 2006; Babetskii et al., 2007; Egert and Kocenda, 2007; Černý and Koblas, 2008; Gilmore et al., 2008; Kocenda and Egert, 2011). In comparison, the studies for the stock markets co-movements in South Eastern Europe are just a few. Kenourgios and Samitas (2011) use conventional test, regime-switching co-integration tests and Monte Carlo simulation to analyze long-run relationships among five Southeastern European (SEE) stock markets (Turkey, Romania, Bulgaria, Croatia, Serbia), the United States and three developed European markets (UK, Germany, Greece), during the period 2000–2009. The authors find enough evidence for a long-run cointegrating relationship between the SEE markets within the region and globally. Gradojevic and Dobardzic (2013) use frequency domain approach to examine the causal relationship between the returns on major indexes of Croatia, Slovenia, Hungary and Germany and the return of the main Serbian index. The results reveal that there is a predominant effect of the Croatian and Slovenian indexes on Serbian stock exchange index across a range of frequencies. Applying GARCH models, Horvath and Petrovski (2013) examine the stock market co-movements between Western and Central Europe (the Czech Republic, Hungary and Poland) on one hand and South Eastern Europe (Croatia, Macedonia and Serbia) on the other hand in the period 2006–2011. The results show that the degree of co-movements is much higher for Central Europe than for South Eastern Europe.

Stoica and Diaconașu (2013) find out the existence of more than one cointegration vectors signifies comovements and linkages for the CEE analysed markets, indicating a stationary long-run relationship. In their study, no dramatic shock was detected in stock market dynamics after the expansion of Vienna Stock Exchange, but still the findings highlighted an increased integration between it and CEE markets in the second subperiod. Additionally, the increasing response to the arrival of price innovations from Austria is registered only in the case of EU markets.

Syllignakis and Kouretas (2010) reveal that the financial linkages between the CEE markets and the world markets increased with the beginning of the EU accession process and also conclude that the global financial crisis of 2007–2009 caused a slowdown in the convergence process. Syriopoulos and Roumpis (2009) note that the Balkan stock markets are seen to exhibit time-varying correlations as a peer group, although correlations with the mature markets remain relatively modest.

A large number of existing studies establishes that due to increasing similarity of returns of different capital markets, the benefits of international diversification of portfolios have gradually faded (Gilmore and McManus, 2004; Aggarwal and Kyaw, 2004; Darrat and Zhong, 2005; Longin and Solnik, 2001). All things considered, stronger integration of financial markets in the presence of internationalization may reduce the power and advantage of diversification; nonetheless, the dissemination of information across financial markets is vital for portfolio managers to construct optimal portfolios. It is further apparent that stock markets have become increasingly important as a source of raising funds for public companies in CEE countries (Stoica el al., 2015).

Gradojevic and Dobardzic (2013) find substantial causality interactions at stock returns at various frequencies between stock market indices in Croatia, Slovenia relative to the returns of Serbian index Belex 15.

In order to assess the impact of the 2008 financial crisis on the interconnection among the SEE stock markets (Macedonian, Croatian, Slovenian, Serbian, and Bulgarian) Zdravkovski (2016) finds out no evidence of cointegration between studied markets during the pre- and post-crisis periods. However, during the 2008 financial crisis, the empirical findings support the existence of three co-integration vectors. This means that the recent global financial crisis and the subsequent euro crisis strengthened the connection between the investigated stock markets. Furthermore, the analysis reveals that during periods of financial turmoil, the Macedonian stock market is positively and actively influenced by the Croatian and Serbian markets. A significant implication of these results is that the integration between SEE stock markets tends to alter over time, particularly during stages of financial disturbances.

Analyzing the Bulgarian and Serbian capital markets, taking into account the 2008 crisis Simeonov (2015) points out that even similarities between two economies, their markets show different reaction to the effects of the crisis. Despite the normally highly volatile capital markets the Serbian investment activity is more vital and more optimistic, than the Bulgarian, which supports the real sector and the economy, as whole. While, the investors on the BSE-Sofia are expressively disposed to undervalue the economic activity, they have continued to behave markedly timorous since 2008. The last fact is a result partially of the naive optimism, spread by the end of 2007.

Todorov (2017) concludes that Bulgaria is characterizing by ineffective money market which stays under the equilibrium levels during stagnation. In his research he indicates about simulating economic growth by increasing money supply and improving the efficiency of Bulgarian capital market. Studding the impact of 2008 financial crisis on the efficiency of the capital markets of Central and Eastern European (CEE) countries Tsenkov (2015) finds differences in market reaction of two of studied markets in the comparison with the rest CEE markets. The Bulgarian and the Romanian indices show disposition for faster and more sensitive reaction to negative market impulses, typical for the Crisis Period, in contrast to a moderate incorporation of the positive market impulses specific to the Pre-crisis Period. The incorporation of the market information by Bulgarian SOFIX during Crisis Period is so accelerated that when it becomes publicly available much of the content is already included in the values of SOFIX under the form of strongly followed market trend. This type of reaction is opposite to the behavior from other CEE indices which follows more sustainable market trends during the pre-crisis period and gives much lower significance of the new market information. This market behavior has changed during the Crisis Period, demonstrating an enhanced response only to the short-term market fluctuations. During the Post-crisis Period the Bulgarian and the Romanian indices are showing predisposition to the short-term market trends. This is opposite to the other CEE indices which tend to form and pursue longer-term market trends.

Yang et al (2004) explores contagion effects and information transmission channels between nine stock markets- Hong Kong, Indonesia, Korea, Malaysia, Thailand, Phillipiness, Singapore, Taiwan and Japan) by applying VAR methodology. He tries to reveal interactions between the aforementioned markets during a crisis period. Shachmurove (2005) reveals the interaction between markets in the Middle East, namely Egypt, Israel, Jordan, Lebanon, Morocco, Oman and Turkey. The applied methodology is VAR model. The results expose that none of the explored financial markets is independent.

1.2. Research Methodology

Before proceeding the econometric analysis of the returns of stock market indexes, we should analyze the graphical dynamic of the explored indexes and their return during the explored period. Their dynamic is revealed in Appendixes 1. It is proved that all graphs expose volatility clusters, especially expressed between the time period of 2007-2009. We observe almost the same dynamic for all of the explored capital markets. Only for the Greek index ATHEX we observe more expressed volatility clusters at the end of the explored period. It may due to the sovereign debt crisis in Greece.

> **Augmented Dickey –Fuller (ADF) test**

According to Tanchev (2016): "Before proceeding to the election of the econometric method, it is necessary to apply a test to establish the stationarity". The null hypothesis of the Augmented Dickey and Fuller (ADF) is non-stationary. The Augmented Dickey-Fuller unit root tests is performed on each series. The tests reject the non-stationary null hypothesis for the stock price index at 1 %, 5 % and 10% significance level for all monthly stock returns at level.

The Augmented Dickey-Fuller (ADF) test constructs a parametric correction for higher-order correlation by assuming that the y series follows an AR (p) process and adding p lagged difference terms of the dependent variable y to the right-hand side of the test regression:

$$\Delta y_t = \alpha y_{t-1} + x_t' \delta + \beta_1 \Delta y_{t-1} + \beta_2 \Delta y_{t-2} + ... + \beta_p \Delta y_{t-p} + v_t \qquad (1)$$

> **Descriptive Statistics**

Table I. Descriptive Statistics for SEE stock market indices

	RATHEX	RBELEX	RBET	RBIFX	RBIRS	RBIST	RCROBEX	RMBI	RMONEX	RSBITOP	RSOFIX
Mean	-0.010485	-0.003972	0.003449	-0.006677	-0.003949	0.009159	0.000679	0.004200	0.011761	-0.004325	-0.002579
Median	0.002666	0.003293	0.011076	-0.012899	-0.008940	0.007646	0.000828	-0.009416	-0.000576	0.000220	-0.000127
Maximum	0.222195	0.276658	0.236225	0.284238	0.307819	0.258045	0.329743	0.418677	0.449368	0.160444	0.310345
Minimum	-0.312754	-0.398026	-0.377969	-0.210969	-0.256846	-0.210731	-0.395540	-0.376864	-0.325570	-0.195710	-0.509278
Std. Dev.	0.096368	0.094793	0.090531	0.076111	0.068390	0.082279	0.086153	0.105123	0.114887	0.059442	0.091216
Skewness	-0.386752	-0.608950	-0.933076	0.776436	0.870484	-0.044665	-0.604120	0.793063	0.739286	-0.466496	-1.320319
Kurtosis	3.576876	6.222918	6.167721	5.705056	7.919202	3.212425	8.604285	6.651975	6.024136	4.259510	11.44921
Jarque-Bera	5.043432	59.84701	73.21697	52.69735	147.4932	0.287648	178.0342	85.86888	61.37935	11.66999	424.4611
Probability	0.080322	0.000000	0.000000	0.000000	0.000000	0.866040	0.000000	0.000000	0.000000	0.002923	0.000000
Sum	-1.363014	-0.480607	0.448319	-0.867978	-0.513333	1.190637	0.088238	0.546046	1.528968	-0.493062	-0.335241

Sum Sq. Dev.	1.197989	1.078279	1.057267	0.747288	0.603357	0.873308	0.957490	1.425567	1.702668	0.399263	1.073321
Observations	130	121	130	130	130	130	130	130	130	114	130

Source: Authors' calculations.

Table I shows the descriptive statistics of the monthly returns for each SEE stock index. We can assume that the Turkish and Montenegrin markets, offers, on average the highest return over the examined period (0,009% and 0,012% respectively). On the other hand, the mean excess return is lower in Greece, Serbia, Bosna and Herzegovina, Banja Luka, Slovenia and Bulgaria. These results confirm previously established results (Stoica and Diaconasu, 2013). The lower standard deviation values indicates that the SEE capital markets exhibit lower volatility, but the highest value is registered for Montenegro. Most of the analyzed index series (7 of the 11 SEE indices) are negatively skewed (except from Bosna and Herzegovina, Banja Luka, Macedonia and Montenegro). There is a higher probability for investors to get negative returns from Bulgaria rather than positive returns due to the highest negative skewness value (-1.32). The kurtosis values of all indices returns are larger than the value of normal distribution (the kurtosis of the normal distribution is 3), indicating that big shocks are more likely to be present for this markets. The Jarque–Bera test (test for normality) rejects normality of distribution of the analyzed markets, which means that all indices exhibit significant departures from normality.

> **Correlation**

Correlation is any of a broad class of statistical relationships involving dependence, though in common usage it most often refers to the extent to which two variables have a linear relationship with each other.

The population correlation coefficient $\hat{\rho}(X,Y)$ between two random variables X and Y is defined as:

$$\hat{\rho}(X,Y) = \frac{\hat{\sigma}(X,Y)}{(\hat{\sigma}(X,X).\hat{\sigma}(Y,Y))^{1/2}} \qquad (2)$$

A correlation coefficient is a number that quantifies a type of correlation and dependence, meaning statistical relationships between two or more values in fundamental statistics

> **VAR methodology**

The technique of Correlation Analysis is a technique, related with some of the following limitations: it estimates the contemporous relationship between the variables, but VAR methodology is a procedure that gives useful insights for lagged links (Patonov, 2016). The vector autoregression (VAR) is commonly used for forecasting systems of interrelated time series and for analyzing the dynamic impact of random disturbances on the system of variables. The VAR approach sidesteps the need for structural modeling by treating every endogenous variable in the system as a function of the lagged values of all of the endogenous variables in the system.

The mathematical representation of a VAR is:

$$y_t = A_1 y_{t-1} + ... + A_p y_{t-p} + B x_t + \varepsilon_t \tag{3}$$

where y_t is a k vector of endogenous variables, x_t is a d vector of exogenous variables, $A_1,...,A_p$ and B are matrices of coefficients to be estimated, and ε_t is a vector of innovations that may be contemporaneously correlated but are uncorrelated with their own lagged values and uncorrelated with all of the right-hand side variables.

Since only lagged values of the endogenous variables appear on the right-hand side of the equations, simultaneity is not an issue and OLS yields consistent estimates. Moreover, even though the innovations ε_t may be contemporaneously correlated, OLS is efficient and equivalent to GLS since all equations have identical regressors. VAR model is a parameter estimation method. Applying VAR model, we reveal possible relations between current and past values of the explored variables. We apply this model, within the framework of a vector autoregression (VAR) model, to examine the dynamics of interdependency between the reference SEE capital markets and developing SEE capital markets. The most important advantage of VAR models is that they provide an opportunity to investigate the reaction of each national stock market to its own price shocks and the price innovations from the reference capital market as well (Stoica and Diaconașu, 2013).

The econometric models have undergone diagnosis analyses for testing their statistical properties, the main steps taken being:

I. Testing for stationarity of the variables;
II. Choosing the most appropriate lag length of the VAR model;
III. Testing the stability of VAR;
IV. Testing for autocorrelations, heteroskedasticity of residual terms and checking for their normal distribution.

We apply variance decomposition and impulse- response function in order to reveal market integration and interaction of SEE capital markets.

To estimate the VAR model we have defined as endogenous variables the returns of each index-the Bulgarian *SOFIX*, the Banja Luka *BIRS*, the Sarajevo *BIFX*, the Greek *Athex Composite Share Price Index (ACSP)*, the Macedonian *MBI10*, the Romanian *BET*, the Serbian *BELEX15*, the Croatian *CROBEX*, the Slovenian *SBI TOP*, the Turkish *BIST100* and the *Montenegrin* MONEX and as exogenous variables the past values (2 lags) of the same variables. The lag-length of VAR is determined by the use of information criteria – Akaike's information criteria (AIC) and Schwarz information criterion (SIC). The Akaike Information Criterion and the Schwarz information criterion (SIC) are tools to select the best model, and we chose the lag that minimizes the AIC and the SIC value. As a best model, we accept the one, in which AIC and SIC's statistics possess lowest values (Table II).

Table II. VAR Order Selection Criteria

Lag	AIC	SIC
0	-29.72709	-26.45069
1	-30.56166	-27.24492
2	-31.83495*	-28.47787*
3	-29.85167	-20.45425
4	-30.64728	-18.20952
5	-30.36653	-15.88843
6	-29.49035	-13.97191
7	-30.24189	-13.68311
8	-29.16045	-16.56133

Source: Authors' calculations.

The stability condition of a VAR is that the characteristic equation roots of the estimated coefficients matrix of VAR should be inside the unit circle (Graph 1). All modulus are smaller than one and this means that the system is stationary. The stability of a system assumes that the shocks are transient and disappear after a certain period of time, and their lack of steadiness implies that certain results, such as the standard errors for the impulse-response function, are not valid (Geamănu, 2014). According to tests, the estimated VAR is stationary.

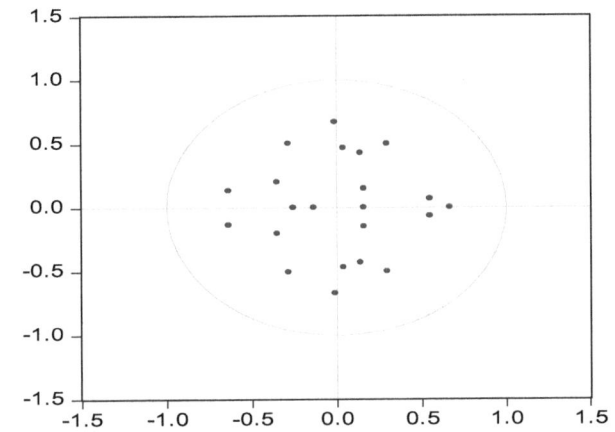

Graph 1: Inverse Roots of AR Characteristic Polynomial
Source: Authors' results

In order to see if there is any autocorrelation, we use Lagrange Multiplier (Table III).

Table III. VAR Residual Serial Correlation LM Tests

Lags	LM-Stat	Probability
1	149.4488	0.0605
2	129.9325	0.2732
3	148.6294	0.0547

Source: Authors' results

The null hypothesis that **H0: no serial correlation at lag order h** is confirmed. This means that it does not exist autocorrelations in first, second and third order and the applied VAR model may be considered as an appropriate one to capture the dynamics and interactions between explored capital markets. The White Heteroskedasticity test to detect the existence of heteroskedasticity (the lack of a constant variance) is applied. The test results are satisfactory, the assumptions of the existence of autocorrelation and existence of homoskedasticity can be rejected at the conventional 5% significant level (Table III, Appendix II).

We apply the Lutkepol test to check the normality of the series (Appendix III). Although small number of the errors do not have a normal distribution, we chose to ignore this problem considering the appropriate models in terms of theory, and the lack of normality does not mean that the model is invalid, but only that there are other variables which explain the model (Geamănu, 2014).

1.3. Research Data

In chapter one, we examine the co-movement of the SEE capital markets using correlation and VAR analysis. Throughout this study it is aimed to reveal that none of the analysed markets is absolutely independent, even though the interrelationships are not so significant. The indices under examination are eleven indices represent all capital markets of South East Europe: the Bulgarian *SOFIX*, the Banja Luka *BIRS*, the Sarajevo *BIFX*, the Greek *Athex Composite Share Price Index (ACSP)*, the Macedonian *MBI10*, the Romanian *BET*, the Serbian *BELEX15*, the Croatian *CROBEX*, the Slovenian *SBI TOP*, the Turkish *BIST100* and the *Montenegrin* MONEX. The stock exchanges of SEE can be divided into two groups in the context of their development, using the stock market capitalization as a criterion (Table V). According to Stavrova (2017): "The process of global financial and economic development have reached a varying degree…" The first group contains the emerging markets – Bulgaria, Romania, Banja Luka and Sarajevo (Bosnia and Herzegovina), Serbia, Montenegro, Macedonia, Slovenia and the second one – reference capital markets – Croatia, Turkey and Greece (Table IV and Table V). Daily closing prices of eleven SEE market indices were available on the Stock Exchanges' websites of the investigated countries. The data range is 1st January 2005 to 4th November 2015. We use the values of the returns of the indices with a monthly frequency. We calculate the percentage change between the opening value of the index on the first working day of month *(Vt)* and the opening value on the first working day of next month *(Vt+1)*, or:

$$R_t = \frac{V_{t+1} - V_t}{V_t} \tag{4}$$

Table IV. Analyzed stock exchanges, indices and a number of observations

Country	Stock exchange	Index
Bulgaria	Bulgarian Stock Exchange	SOFIX
Bosnia and Herzegovina	Banja Luka stock exchange	BIRS
Bosnia and Herzegovina	Sarajevo stock exchange	BIFX
Greece	Athens Stock Exchange	Athex Composite Share Price
Macedonia	Macedonian Stock Exchange	MBI10
Romania	Bucharest Stock Exchange	BET

Serbia	Belgrade Stock Exchange	BELEX15
Croatia	Zagreb Stock Exchange	CROBEX
Slovenia	Ljubljana Stock Exchange	SBI TOP
Turkey	Borsa Istanbul	BIST100
Montenegro	Montenegro Stock Exchange	MONEX

Notes for Table 1: Southeast Europe includes 10 countries: Bulgaria, Bosnia and Herzegovina (two capital markets-Sarajevo and Banja Luka), Greece, Macedonia, Romania, Serbia, Croatia, Slovenia, Turkey and Montenegro.
Source: Author's calculations.

Table V. Market capitalization of SEE capital markets for 2011

SEE capital markets	Market capitalization (US$)
Country	**2011 (billion)**
Bulgaria	8,253.25 US$
Croatia	22,558.38 US$
Greece	33,778.89 US$
Banja Luka (Bosnia and Herzegovina)	2,601.39 US$
Sarajevo (Bosnia and Herzegovina)	2,263.89 US$
Montenegro	3,509.11 US$
Romania	14,023.92 US$
Serbia	4,055.58 US$
Slovenia	6,325.86 US$
Turkey	197,074.46 US$
Macedonia	580.36 US$

Notes for Table 2: The total market capitalization of each capital market is for 2011 (approximately in the middle of the examined period 2005-2015).
Source: The websites of the SEE stock exchanges.

Table VI. Developing and reference capital markets (according to the market capitalization)

Developing SEE capital markets	Reference SEE capital markets
Bulgaria	***Greece***
Banja Luka (Bosnia and Herzegovina)	***Croatia***
Sarajevo (Bosnia and Herzegovina)	***Turkey***
Macedonia	

Montenegro	
Romania	
Serbia	
Slovenia	

Notes for Table 3: Median market capitalization is US $ 6,325.86 billion.
Source: Author's calculations.

1.4. Empirical results for the integration of Southeast European Capital Markets

➢ **Stationary**

Table VII. Estimating results of *Augmented Dickey –Fuller (ADF) test*

Country/ Indices	Parameters		Stock index Return*
Bulgaria	**ADF statistic**		-7.597629
	Critical Values	**1%**	-3.481623
		5%	-2.883930
		10%	-2.578788
	p-value		*0.0000*
Croatia	**ADF statistic**		-10.75016
	Critical Values	**1%**	-3.481623
		5%	-2.883930
		10%	-2.578788
	p-value		*0.0000*
Greece	**ADF statistic**		-9.675144
	Critical Values	**1%**	-3.481623
		5%	-2.883930
		10%	-2.578788
	p-value		*0.0000*
Macedonia	**ADF statistic**		-6.088729
	Critical Values	**1%**	-3.600987
		5%	-2.935001
		10%	-2.605836
	p-value		*0.0000*
Montenegro	**ADF statistic**		-5.213145
	Critical Values	**1%**	-3.610453
		5%	-2.938987
		10%	-2.607932
	p-value		*0.0001*
Romania	**ADF statistic**		-9.291294
	Critical Values	**1%**	-3.481623
		5%	-2.883930
		10%	-2.578788

		p-value		0.0000
Slovenia	ADF statistic			-7.233281
	Critical Values	1%		-3.488063
		5%		-2.886732
		10%		-2.580281
	p-value			0.0000
Turkey	ADF statistic			-9.430183
	Critical Values	1%		-3.496346
		5%		-2.890327
		10%		-2.582196
	p-value			0.0000
Serbia	ADF statistic			-4.391736
	Critical Values	1%		-3.486551
		5%		-2.886074
		10%		-2.579931
	p-value			0.0005
Banja Luka	ADF statistic			-7.030134
	Critical Values	1%		-3.481623
		5%		-2.883930
		10%		-2.578788
	p-value			0.0000
Sarajevo	ADF statistic			-5.970411
	Critical Values	1%		-3.482035
		5%		-2.884109
		10%		-2.578884
	p-value			0.0000

*All of the stock index returns are stationary at level.
Source: Authors' calculations.

Before analyzing the co-movement of the SEE financial markets, the Augmented Dickey-Fuller (ADF) test is applied to examine the stationary properties of the return series. The null hypothesis of ADF test is that the series has a unit root (non-stationary process). It can be seen from the above table, the series **are stationary at level**.

> **Correlation analysis**

Table VIII. *Correlation matrix of examined SEE market indices*

	ACSP	BELEX15	BET	BIFX	BIRS	BIST100	CROBEX	MBI10	MONEX	SBITOP	SOFIX
ACSP	**1.000000**										
BELEX15	0.450656	**1.000000**									
BET	0.642541	0.533182	**1.000000**								
BIFX	0.289116	0.658350	0.327432	**1.000000**							

BIRS	0.159478	0.536066	0.212359	0.524708	**1.000000**					
BIST100	0.516566	0.299001	0.546841	0.275759	0.167652	**1.000000**				
CROBEX	0.507915	0.669970	0.608768	0.479733	0.368159	0.481318	**1.000000**			
MBI10	0.340126	0.653152	0.385513	0.423698	0.470494	0.234876	0.600676	**1.000000**		
MONEX	0.345074	0.685317	0.310752	0.540538	0.504158	0.343549	0.679181	0.690677	**1.000000**		
SBITOP	0.536818	0.576229	0.490587	0.500012	0.287006	0.390038	0.542098	0.547407	0.467569	**1.000000**	
SOFIX	0.515429	0.603714	0.661221	0.370920	0.271405	0.406721	0.616263	0.379637	0.350571	0.549255	**1.000000**

Source: Author's calculations.

In order to examine the co-movement of the SEE capital markets the correlation analysis is applied. Analyzing the results of the correlation matrix the major conclusions for the harmonization of the examined indices in the region. The correlation matrix is presented in Table 5. The Serbian index BELEX15 registers the highest correlations with the other examined indices. In contrast, the least connected capital market in the region is that of Banja Luka, considering the lowest values of registered correlation coefficients. In addition, the Montenegrin index MONEX is relatively closely correlated with the Serbian index BELEX15 (0.685317), the Croatian index CROBEX (0.679181) and the Macedonian index MBI10 (0.690677), which can be attributed to the existing integration between these financial markets with close and similar development and characteristics. Additionally, these capital markets face similar challenges and problems - corruption, judicial independence, law enforcement, shadow economy, limited number of foreign investors and the issue offree movement of capital. The Croatian index CROBEX is predictably high associated with BELEX15 (0.669970), BET (0.608768), MONEX (0.679181), MBI10 (0.690677) and SOFIX (0.616263) due to the symmetric market shocks on these capital markets, and their close economic development and growth. It was proved that the index BIST100 of the reference Turkish capital market registered a low or moderate correlation with the other indices in the region, which means that the market dynamics of this market does not affect the other financial markets in SEE. In addition, the Turkish market show relatively high correlation (compared to other SEE capital markets SEE) with reference Greek capital market (0.516566).

On the other hand, the countries that are not part of the European Union (EU) - Montenegro, Macedonia, Bosnia and Herzegovina (Sarajevo and Banja Luka) are characterized with moderate or low values of correlation coefficients, probably due to different market dynamics during the financial crisis of 2008. Additionally, for reference capital markets in the region, namely Turkey, Greece and Croatia is registered low or moderate positive correlation, suggesting that there are not leading and dominant financial market to influence the market dynamics of all other SEE indices. Several additions can be made here. Firstly, the Greek market is weakly correlated with all developing SEE capital markets (Macedonia, Serbia, Montenegro, Slovenia, Banja Luka, Sarajevo, Bulgaria), with the exception of the Romanian one, considering the low positive correlation coefficients. Secondly, the Turkish capital market has shown a low correlation with all emerging markets in the region. In addition, the Slovenian index is characterized by a low or moderate relationship with other SEE equity markets. A possible explanation for such weak correlation between the Slovenian capital market and the other SEE markets can be sought in the overtaking and rapid development of this market and the growth in market turnover in the last few years as a result of the introduction of new financial instruments (derivatives), attracting international portfolio investors, as well as local institutional investors.

Bulgaria is relatively synchronized with other countries in the region considering the highest correlation with Serbia (0.603714), Romania (0.661221) and Croatia (0.616263). It can be assumed that this is due to the symmetrical shocks to which the Bulgarian and other capital markets are exposed, as well as to the geographic proximity between these countries and the correspondingly intensive flows of capital assets between them.

> **VAR model**

Graph 2 and Graph 3 show the estimated results of the applied VAR model, where only statistically significant values and interrelations are exposed. Graph 2 includes the interactions between reference and emerging capital markets. Graph 3 exposes the statistically significant relations only between emerging markets.

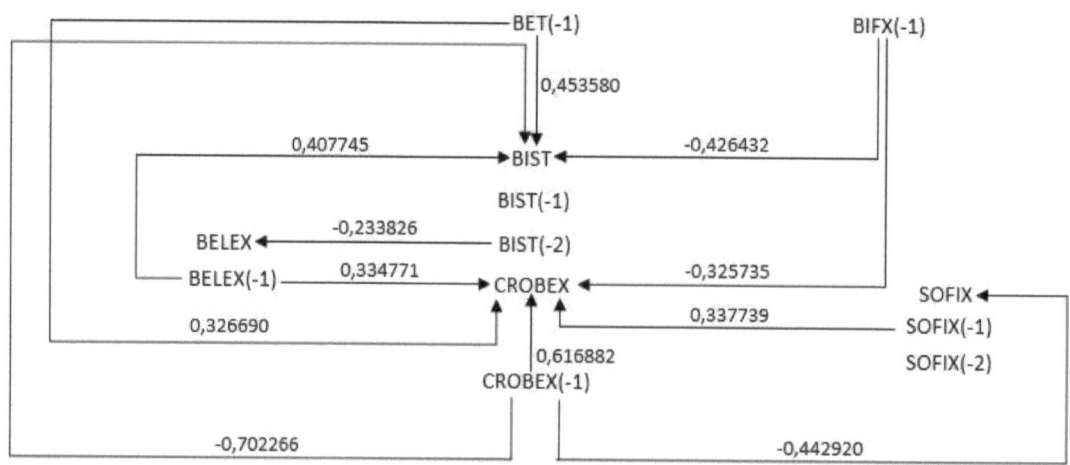

Graph 2. VAR results for interactions between reference and developing capital markets

Source: Authors' calculations.
Notes: They are exposed only statistically significant relationships.

For BIST returns we have found that the values of t- statistics associated with BELEX (-1), BET (-1), BIFX (-1) and CROBEX (-1) are higher than 2 (in absolute values), so it means that these observations are statistically relevant to explain the current values of BIST. Consequently, we may conclude that the returns of BELEX, BET, BIFX and CROBEX with one lag have impact on the current of BIST returns. We observe positive influence over BIST from BELEX (-1) and BET (-1) with coefficient values equal to (0.407745) and (0.453580). This means that an increase in the values of the aforementioned indexes indicates increase in BIST values. The strongest negative interaction is revealed between the current return of BIST and CROBEX (-1). The coefficient value is equal to (-0.702266). This indicates that in average when CROBEX returns from a month before increase with 1 pp the current returns from BIST decreases 70.22%, assuming that the rest remains constant. This leads to the conclusion that the strongest negative relationship is proved between two of the reference capital markets. The coefficient value of BIFX (-1) is negative with weight of the coefficient (-0.426432), either. This indicates for inverse relation between BIST returns and BIFX (-1). BIST (-2) returns influence negatively to BELEX current returns with coefficient value (-0.233826). In direct comparison between both interactions reference-developing capital markets and vise- versa, the current BELEX returns incorporate the information from BIST with two lags and the relation is inverse. The Turkish BIST100 incorporates the information from BELEX with one lag and the relation is straightforward. As an explanation for the aforementioned results, we may point out the higher information efficiency of Turkish BIST100. It is proved by the faster information incorporation of BELEX values and the higher value of the coefficient (0.407745).

For CROBEX returns we have found that the values of t- statistics associated with BELEX (-1), BET (-1), BIFX (-1), CROBEX (-1) are higher than 2 (in absolute values), so it means that these observations are statistically relevant to explain the current values of CROBEX. Consequently, we may conclude that the returns of BELEX, BET, BIFX, and CROBEX with one lag have impact on the current of CROBEX. From the lag period, we should mention that CROBEX current returns incorporate the information flows from the aforementioned indexes fast. The coefficient values indicate for moderate interaction between these financial markets. CROBEX (-1) and BIFX (-1) have negative signs of their coefficients equal to (-0.616882) and (-0.325735). The strongest relation we observe for the past values of CROBEX returns for 61.68 %. BELEX (-1), BET (-1) and SOFIX (-1) influence CROBEX with the following coefficient values (0.334771), (0.326690) and (0.337739). This indicates that in average when BELEX (-1), BET (-1) and SOFIX (-1) returns from a month before increase with 1 pp the current returns from CROBEX increase respectively with 33.47%, 32.66% and 33.77% assuming that the rest remains constant. We observe bilateral relationship between CROBEX and SOFIX. For SOFIX returns, we have found that the coefficient value of CROBEX (-1) is statistically significant. It is equal to (-0.422920). This relationship indicates for fast information incorporation of both markets with one lag. The influence of CROBEX (-1) in the returns of SOFIX is stronger than the influence of SOFIX (-1) in the current returns of CROBEX (0.337739). The Romanian BET current returns are determined by CROBEX (-1), either. The coefficient value is equal to (-0.549878) with negative sign. This indicates that in average when CROBEX returns from a month before increases by 1pp the current returns from BET decrease 54.98%, assuming that the rest remains constant. We observe higher coefficient values of CROBEX (-1) for the Romanian BET returns than the Bulgarian SOFIX with difference equal to 12.69%.

From the exposed interactions in Graph 2, we reveal significant relations between capital markets of SEE independent of the separation of reference and developing capital markets. The results reveal that for the reference Greek capital market, we do not register significant relationships. Turkish BIST and the Croatian CROBEX are determined by the dynamic of indexes of the developing stock markets. The results of VAR model confirm the ones of the correlation test that BELEX 15 is high correlated with the markets from the group, especially for the reference ones. The Bulgarian capital market indicates significant bilateral relationship with the Croatian capital market. It is revealed that the Bulgarian, Romanian and Serbian capital markets are interacting with the reference capital markets from SEE group.

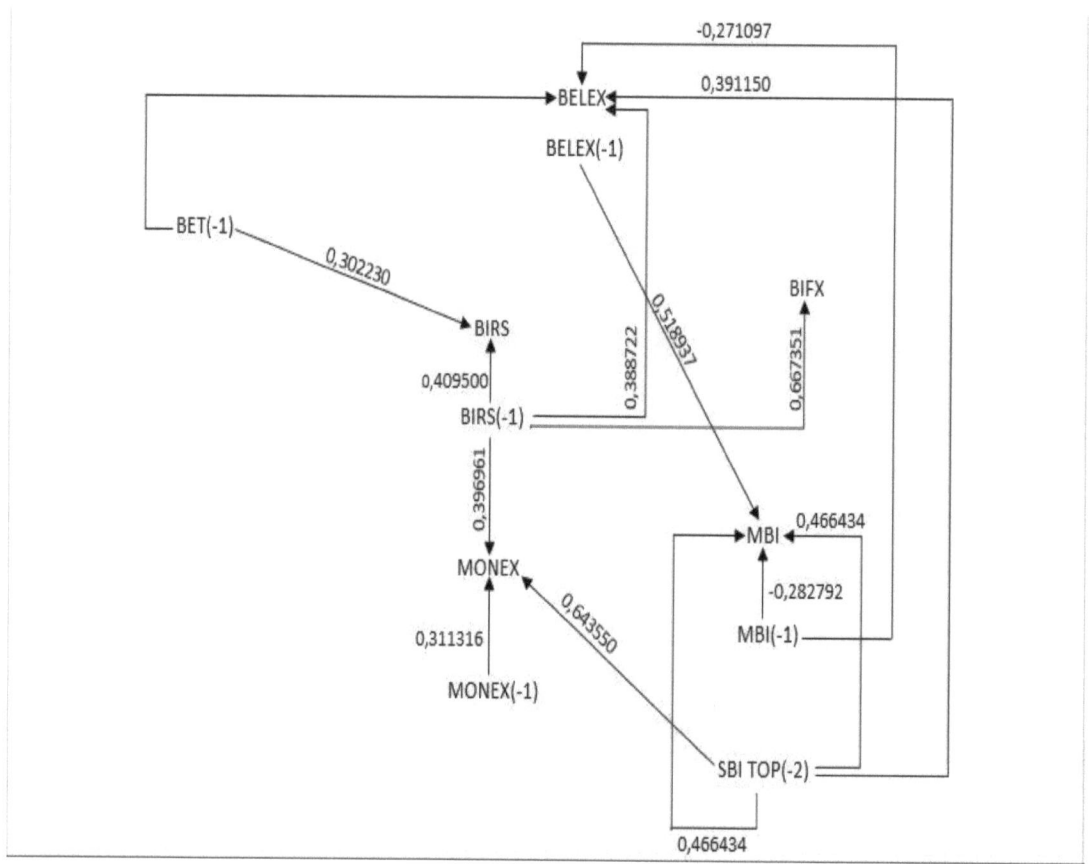

Graph 3. VAR results for interactions between developing capital markets of SEE group
Source: Authors' calculations.
Notes: They are exposed only statistically significant relationships.

For BELEX returns, we have proved that the values of t- statistics associated with BET (-1), BIRS (-1), BIST (-2), MBI (-1) and SBI TOP (-2) are statistically significant. Consequently, we may conclude that the returns of BET, BIRS and MBI with one lag and the returns of SBI TOP and BIST with two lags have impact on the current of BELEX returns. Positive influence we reveal for BET (-1) (0.473961), BIRS (-1) (0.388722) and SBI TOP (0.391150). These results indicate that an increase in the values of the aforementioned indexes indicates increase in the values of BELEX. The strongest interaction is revealed between BET (-1) and BELEX with coefficient value equal to (0.473961). This indicates that in average when BET returns from the month before increase by 1 pp the current returns of BELEX increase 47.39 %, assuming that the rest remains constant. Negative influence, we reveal for MBI (-1) and BIST (-2) with coefficient values respectively equal to (-0.271097) and (-0.233826) (Graph 1). The significant interactions confirm the results from the correlation analysis, namely The Serbian capital market is highly determined by the other markets of the SEE group. The coefficient value of BELEX (-1) is statistically significant in determining the current returns of MBI 10. Its value is equal to (0.518937). This indicates that in average when BELEX returns from the month before increase by 1 pp the current returns of Macedonian MBI increase 51.89 %, assuming that the rest remains constant.

BIRS current returns are determined by its past values BIRS (-1) and BET (-1) with positive coefficient values respectively equal to (0.409500) and (0.302230). The past values of BIRS with one lag- BIRS (-1) determine the current returns of BIFX with positive coefficient equal to (0.667351) and the current values of MONEX with lower coefficient value equal to (0.396961). The capital market of Banja Luka is small and limited so these characteristics may explain the lack of significant relations between BIRS and the capital markets indexes of the SEE group.

The dynamics of the Macedonian index MBI 10 is determined by the dynamic of the following indexes: BELEX (-1) (0.518937), MBI (-1) (-0.282792) and the Slovenian SBI TOP (-2) (0.466434). As we have mentioned before, the dynamic of the Serbian BELEX has the strongest influence for the MBI 10. The dynamic of the Slovenian SBI TOP (-2) is in positive relationship with MBI 10. The Macedonian MBI incorporates the information from the Slovenian index more slowly than the information from the Serbian capital market. It is proved by the lag interdependences.

For MONEX returns, we have proved that the values of t- statistics associated with BET (-1), BIRS (-1), MONEX (-1) and SBI TOP (-2) are statistically significant. Consequently, we may conclude that the returns of BET, BIRS and MONEX with one lag and the returns of SBI TOP with two lags have impact on the current of MONEX returns. We observe that the information from the Slovenian capital market is not incorporated in the values of the Macedonian index and MONEX returns as quickly as the information from the other statistically significant dynamic of stock market indexes. The strongest positive influence is revealed from the SBI TOP with coefficient value equal to (0.643550). The coefficient value of the Romanian BET is positive and it is equal to (0.386703). The past values of MONEX-MONEX (-1) possess the lowest influence from the statistically significant indexes that determine the dynamic of MONEX. It is equal to (0.311316). For MONEX returns, we have proved that the dynamic of BET (-1), BIRS (-1), MONEX (-1) and SBI TOP (-2) have positive influence for the dynamic of MONEX.

We should mention that for the Slovenian capital market we do not register significant capital markets from SEE group to determine its dynamic.

By Graph 3, we reveal the significant relations only between developing capital markets in SEE group. We prove moderate degree of interaction between them. The dynamics of BIFX, BIRS, MBI and MONEX are not determined by the dynamic of the reference capital markets from SEE group. They interact and incorporate the information between themselves.

Table IX. Forecast Error of Variance Decomposition

Country	*Days*	*Own*	*Greece*	*Croatia*	*Turkey*
Bulgaria	3	36.68	25.40	3.77	0.59
	5	34.27	25.25	3.57	0.57
	10	33.50	25.21	3.60	0.61
Banja Luka	3	64.29	4.12	1.91	1.54
	5	61.49	5.53	1.80	1.56
	10	60.71	5.64	1.78	1.56
Sarajevo	3	40.19	7.83	1.33	1.33
	5	36.50	8.49	1.21	1.35
	10	35.61	8.88	1.18	1.37
Macedonia	3	38.41	1.33	5.79	1.33
	5	35.80	1.35	5.39	1.90
	10	35.04	1.37	5.29	1.90
Montenegro	3	27.28	38.41	8.39	5.68
	5	25.78	35.80	7.94	5.72
	10	25.38	35.04	7.84	5.71
Romania	3	35.04	37.62	8.99	0.05
	5	33.01	36.46	8.68	0.06
	10	32.69	36.05	8.64	0.14
Serbia	3	43.35	23.00	2.70	2.94
	5	40.76	22.08	2.63	3.32
	10	40.23	22.18	2.60	3.33
Slovenia	3	44.94	25.04	2.49	2.54
	5	43.53	25.01	2.39	2.44
	10	42.94	25.20	2.35	2.40

Source: Authors' Calculations

Table IX provides a quantitative measure of short- run dynamic interdependences of the developing capital SEE with the reference capital markets. In this study, we apply Choleski decomposition to orthogonalise the shocks method. So, in Table IX are studied the variance decomposition results of 3-day, 5-day and 10-day horizon ahead forecast error variances of each developing stock market with the reference capital ones.

Table IX suggests that in all countries by day 3 or 5 ahead, the behaviour has settled down to a steady condition. Therefore Table IX suggests that in the most of the analysed countries, the national market price innovations account for more of the error variance while Greek, Croatian and Turkish price innovations account for less of the forecast error variance. These results confirm that the expected returns of the investment in the developing SEE stock markets are determined mainly by country-specific risk factors The implication of the low level of the interactions is that expected returns of the investment in the emerging stock markets should be determined mostly by the country-specific risk factors (Li and Majerowska, 2008; Stoica el al., 2015). The highest shocks that affects the series in the system is observed on the basis till 37.62% of the variation in the returns of analysed indices is caused by the Greek market. The capital markets of Banja Luka, Sarajevo and Macedonia are the ones which are weakly linked and affected by the influence of the reference capital markets. In addition, in the capital markets of Montenegro and Romania the national market price innovations do not account for more of the error variance. They are more influenced by the innovations of the Greek capital market. Bulgarian, Serbian and Slovenian capital markets are determined by their country- specific risk but they are strongly affected by the innovations of the Greek stock market. On the basis that about 0.57-8.99% of the variation in the returns of analysed indices is caused by shocks to Croatian and Turkish markets, indeed the extent of influence of the reference capital markets on the returns of the developing markets in SEE is not weak. Bulgarian and Romanian capital markets are the ones which are influenced by the Turkish innovations in a lowest degree- about 0.05-0.61%. The capital market of Banja Luka is the one which is determined by its own innovations in a stronger value- about 60.71- 64.29% compared to the others explored developing markets in SEE group. The extent of influence of the reference capital markets on the returns of the Banja Luka market is small, indicating a weak integration of Banja Luka market with the reference capital ones in the area.

The implication of the low level of the linkages is that expected returns of the investment in the explored developing stock markets would be determined mainly by the country-specific risk factors (Li and Majerowska, 2008). Five countries appear more sensitive to shocks from the Greek market.

We utilize impulse-response function to address the question of how rapidly events in one variable are transmitted to the others. The advantage of the impulse response function is that it allows "innovation accounting". The impulse response functions show how a particular variable responds to shocks to other variables in the system. In other words, an innovation in a given variable triggers a chain reaction over time in the remaining variables. The impulse response functions allow us to assess these chain reactions. Impulse- response function results can be seen in Appendix V. In these graphs, it is seen that response of series when representing one standard deviation shock of each other. Action and reaction analysis can be seen in graphs. Following a one standard deviation shock to the Greek ATHEX, BELEX and BIRS indicate increase. They increase in short- run period. BIFX and MBI indices respond by a weak increase in short- run period. SBI TOP responds with immediate decrease, the same is the reaction of the Romanian BET. The Bulgarian SOFIX reacts by a weak increase that is followed by a sudden and strong decrease. Following a one standard deviation shock to the Croatian CROBEX, the explored developing capital markets react with a similar dynamic- sudden strong decrease in their values with a following slow increase. The exception of the aforementioned dynamic is the response of SBITOP. The Slovenian capital market reacts with a slow and smooth decrease. We should emphasize that all of the explored developing capital markets from SEE have similar reactions to the shocks and amendments in Croatian market. Following a one standard deviation shock to the Turkish BIST, BIRS and MONEX respond with a sudden decrease followed by short- run increase. We should emphasize that Bulgarian and Romanian capital market respond very weakly to the shocks of Turkish capital market. The reaction of BELEX, BIFX, MBI and SBI TOP is revealed by quick increase followed by a decrease in short- run period.

To conclude the results from VAR model, variance decomposition and impulse response function, we prove significant interactions between capital markets' dynamic from SEE group in two lag period. We prove high degree of integration of the Bulgarian, Romanian and Serbian capital markets among the reference capital markets of this group of countries. It is proved fast degree of information incorporation for reference and developing capital markets from the other members of the group. We should mention that we observe less significant interactions between reference capital markets than the ones between developing. These results confirm the ones from the correlation analysis. The developing capital markets of the explored group are strongly determined by country- specific factors, but five of them are strongly influenced by the Greek innovations. However, the market integration is anticipated to strengthen, as a result of EU expansion, as the implementation of Strategy 2020. These results lead to the argument that investor can benefit, at least in the short run, from diversifying into the SEE equity markets.

CHAPTER TWO: Impact of sentiment indicators on the capital market dynamics and default probability

2.1. Studies on the impact of sentiment indicators on the capital market dynamics and default probability

Sentiment indicators and CDS spreads are in the focus of attention of many researchers. Tang and Jan (2010) reveal that the relationship between the probability of default and investor sentiment depends on the state of the market, namely if it is bullish or bearish. They assume that Conference Board Consumer Confidence Index as a proxy for changes of risk aversion. Tang and Jan (2010) prove that the investor sentiment may be considered as a good and effective instrument for Credit spread prediction. We should mention the investor inattention theory (Easley, O'hara, and Srinivas, 1998; Della Vigna and Pollet, 2009; Cohen and Frazzini, 2008; Barber and Odean, 2008; Duffie and Lando, 2001). The theory claims that limits of human attention affect market prices. DellaVigna and Pollet (2009) prove that reduced investor attention causes less immediate responses to earnings announcements . This measure is based on the assumption that investors with limited attention tend to neglect information about cash profitability, and focus on accounting profitability. They find that this inattention measure significantly predicts long-run stock returns. Hilscher, Pollet, and Wilson (2015) reveal that CDS traders are liquidity traders and are inattentive to news development, in comparison to the informed traders in the equity market. It is proved that credit traders respond faster during the salient news events, such as earnings announcements (Lamont and Frazzini, 2007; Greatrex, 2009). This is proved by Norden and Weber (2004), namely that CDS spreads react faster than the equity returns only during negative rating announcements: CDS incorporate negative information flows fater than the equity returns. Spyrou (2013) has reported that investor sentiment may be an important bond yield determinant for the following period: 2008-2010. Later Spyrou, Galariotis and Makrichoti (2016) have used Economic Sentiment Indicator and ZEW Economic Sentiment Indicator to reveal the investor sentiment influence on credit default swaps spread. They found out that sentiment may play a role in CDS spread determination, albeit limiting. This is why in addition we also employ variables that proxy for behavioral determinants because they may represent investors and economic sentiment.

The connection between sentiment indicators and capital markets dynamics are examined in many studies. Görmüş and Güneş (2010) analyze the effect of Consumer Confidence Index (CCI) on real exchange rate and stock market in Turkey for the period 2002-2008 using econometric techniques. The results from GARCH-M and OLS model show that CCI affect real exchange rate and stock prices. Oprea and Brad (2014) investigate the relationship between the consumer confidence index and the Romanian stock market for the period 2002-2011. They argue that there is a positive correlation between changes in consumer confidence and stock market returns, displaying that individual investor sentiment affects stock prices. In the study conducted by Miljković and Radović (2006) evidence that the Serbian stock market does not show efficiency even in the weak-form of EMH is presented. They find statistically significant levels of autocorrelation in returns with high kurtosis distribution, considerably different from the normal one. Borges (2010) studies stock markets of France, Germany, UK, Greece, Portugal and Spain to check for the presence of random walk for the period from January 1993 to December 2007. Using both parametric and nonparametric tests, he finds evidence of random walk in all six countries for monthly return. Moreover, the hypothesis of random walk was rejected for Portugal and Greece for the daily return. Aga and Kocaman (2011) test the weak form of efficiency for return index-20 in Istanbul Stock Exchange (ISE) for the period 1986-2005. They lead to the conclusion that there is a weak form of efficiency in ISE, which means that the market is weakly efficient if the current time cannot be explained with the past values. Investigating calendar anomalies for five SEE stock markets (Bulgaria, Croatia, Greece, Romania and Turkey) during the period 2000-2008, Georgantopoulos, Kenourgios and Tsamis (2011) find evidence for the existence of three calendar effects (day of the week, turn of the month, time of the month) in both mean and volatility equations for Greece and Turkey, which is consistent to the findings of previous studies. On the other hand, the effects for the three emerging SEE markets are limited and exist only in volatility. Samitas, Kenourgios and Paltalidis (2011) study long-run relationships among five Balkan emerging stock markets (Turkey, Romania, Bulgaria, Croatia, and Serbia), the US and three developed European markets (UK, Germany and Greece) during the period 2000-2006. The results indicate that both domestic and external factors affect the Balkan stock markets, shaping their longrun equilibrium. Overall, they show evidence in favor of significant long-run relations between the Balkan emerging markets within the region and globally. Armeanu and Cioaca (2014) test the EMH in the case of Romania for 01.01.2002 -15.05.2014 using four methods, including GARCH model. They find out that the Romanian capital market is not weak-form efficient. Dragota and Oprea (2014) investigate the Romanian stock market's informational efficiency and find out that the predictability of returns suggest that the Romanian stock market has a low level of efficiency. Furthermore, the impact of new information is more intense before and after its release. Estimating the effect of the World Economic Crisis on the Countries of the Balkan Region Geshkov (2014) finds that the most affected countries are Greece and Bosnia and Herzegovina.

Corredor et al. (2015) examine the effect of investor sentiment on stock returns in three Central European markets: the Czech Republic, Hungary and Poland. The results show that sentiment is a key variable in the prices of stocks traded on these markets and its impact is stronger here than in more developed European markets.

2.2. Research Methodology

We use the models of the GARCH- family models (GARCH (p,q), EGARCH (p,q), TGARCH(p,q) and PGARCH(p,q)) for examining the relationship between public expectations and financial market dynamics, including the additional variables in the models, such as consumer confidence indicator (CCI), industrial confidence indicator (ICI) and inflation expectations (InfExp). The appropriate GARCH model of GARCH-family models for each index is applied to examine the relationship between public expectations and capital market dynamics. Higher order GARCH models, denoted GARCH (q, p) can be estimated by choosing either q or p greater than 1 where q is the order of the autoregressive GARCH terms and p is the order of the moving average ARCH terms.

➢ The representation of the GARCH (q, p) variance is:

$$\sigma_t^2 = \omega + \sum_{j=1}^{q} \beta_j \sigma_{t-j}^2 + \sum_{i=1}^{p} \beta_i \varepsilon_{t-i}^2 \tag{5}$$

➢ The EGARCH or Exponential GARCH model was proposed by Nelson (1991). The specification for the conditional variance is:

$$\log(\sigma_t^2) = \omega + \sum_{j=1}^{q} \beta_j \log(\sigma_{t-j}^2) + \sum_{i=1}^{p} \alpha_i \left| \frac{\varepsilon_{t-i}}{\sigma_{t-i}} \right| + \sum_{k=1}^{r} \gamma_k \frac{\varepsilon_{t-k}}{\sigma_{t-k}} \tag{6}$$

Note that the left-hand side is the log of the conditional variance. This implies that the leverage effect is exponential, rather than quadratic, and that forecasts of the conditional variance are guaranteed to be nonnegative. The presence of leverage effects can be tested by the hypothesis that $\gamma_i < 0$. The impact is asymmetric if $\gamma_i \neq 0$.

➢ The Threshold GARCH (TGARCH) Model - TARCH or Threshold ARCH and Threshold GARCH were introduced independently by Zakoïan (1994) and Glosten, Jaganathan, and Runkle (1993). The generalized specification for the conditional variance is given by:

$$\sigma_t^2 = \omega + \sum_{j=1}^{q} \beta_j \sigma_{t-j}^2 + \sum_{i=1}^{p} \alpha_i \varepsilon_{t-i}^2 + \sum_{k=1}^{r} \gamma_k \varepsilon_{t-k}^2 I_{t-k} \tag{7}$$

where $I_t = 1$ if $\varepsilon_t < 0$ and 0 otherwise.

In this model, good news, $\varepsilon_{t-i} > 0$, and bad news $\varepsilon_{t-i} < 0$, have differential effects on the conditional variance; good news has an impact of α_i, while bad news has an impact of $\alpha_i + \gamma_i$. If $\gamma_i > 0$, bad news increases volatility, and we say that there is a *leverage effect* for the i-th order. If $\gamma_i \neq 0$, the news impact is asymmetric.

➢ The Power GARCH (PGARCH) Model - Taylor (1986) and Schwert (1989) introduced the standard deviation GARCH model, where the standard deviation is modeled rather than the variance. This model, along with several other models, is generalized in Ding et al. (1993) with the Power ARCH specification. In the Power ARCH model, the power parameter δ of the standard deviation can be estimated rather than imposed, and the optional γ parameters are added to capture asymmetry of up to order r:

$$\sigma_t^\delta = \omega + \sum_{j=1}^{q} \beta_j \sigma_{t-j}^\delta + \sum_{i=1}^{p} \alpha_i (|\varepsilon_{t-i}| - \gamma_i \varepsilon_{t-i})^\delta \qquad (8)$$

where $\delta > 0, |\gamma_i| \leq 1$ for $i = 1,....,r, \gamma_i = 0$, for all $i > r$, and $r \leq p.$.

The symmetric model sets $\gamma_i = 0$ for all i. Note that if $\delta = 2$ and $\gamma_i = 0$ for all i, the PARCH model is simply a standard GARCH specification. As in the previous models, the asymmetric effects are present if $\gamma \neq 0$.

2.3. Data research

We will use again the values of the returns of the indices with a monthly frequency. We calculate the percentage change between the opening value of the index on the first working day of month (V_t) and the opening value on the first working day of next month (V_{t+1}), or:

$$R_t = \frac{V_{t+1} - V_t}{V_t} \qquad (9)$$

All data for the values of the consumer confidence indicator (CCI), industrial confidence indicator (ICI) and inflation expectations (InfExp) is available in the database of the Eurostat Statistical Service. Consumer and industrial confidence indicators are indices composed of questions about general conditions for households and firms, respectively.

Consumer confidence (or sentiment) surveys began in the 1950s in the US backed up by the idea that asking the general public about their overall consumption and price expectations, together with purchasing intents, can serve as a viable leading indicator for economic fluctuations. This holds especially true for more developed economies where consumption can take three quarters of total output or even beyond. And it is indeed the case that sentiment data has forecasting capabilities well above and beyond that of standard macroeconomic indicators (Curtin, 2007).

The industrial confidence indicator including key components such as capacity, backlog, orders, and so on, which are then summarized into an overall index.

Inflation expectations data is a question asking the general public if they expect prices to rise faster, rise at the same rate, rise slower, remain the same, or decrease. Additionally, there is not available data for these indicators for Montenegro, Serbia, Bosnia and Herzegovina and

Banja Luka, although in the nearest future these SEE countries should start calculating the public expectation indicators because of the terms of joining the European Union.

2.4. Empirical results for the impact of sentiment indicators on the capital market dynamics and default probability

> **The impact of consumer sentiment on the capital market dynamics**

Table X. Estimating results of GARCH models for the influence of the consumer confidence indicator on the capital market dynamics

Index	The most appropriate GARCH model	CCI (Prob)
SOFIX	PGARCH (1,2) -t	*0.125358* *(0.0113)*
CROBEX	PGARCH (2,1)-t	-0.010476 (0.6703)
ACSP	EGARCH (2,1)-t	-0.011788 (0.8629)
MBI10	EGARCH (1,1)-t	*-0.008110* *(0.0117)*
BET	EGARCH (2,2)-t	*-0.102886* *(0.0047)*
SBITOP	EGARCH (1,2)-t	*-0.053161* *(0.0008)*
BIST100	EGARCH (2,2)-t	0.001895 (0.9213)

Notes for Table X.: The data of the consumer confidence indicator is included in the equation of EGARCH (p,q) or PGARCH (p,q) model.
Source: Author's calculations.

The Table X shows the values of the consumer confidence indicator (CCI) in the equation of EGARCH (p,q) or PGARCH(p,q) model. We should note that for four of the examined indices there are statistically significant values at 5% of CCI. Moreover, the absolute values of CCI are in the range from 0.008110 (MBI10) to 0.125358 (SOFIX). Remarkably, the highest value of CCI is registered for SOFIX, indicating that this sentiment indicator has a relatively significant influence on the dynamics of Bulgarian capital market. Here, we should specify that statistically significant consumer confidence indicators are calculated only for the emerging SEE capital markets – Bulgarian (0.125358), Slovenian (-0.053161), Macedonian (-0.008110) and Romanian (-0.102886). One of the possible explanation of the registered insignificant values of CCI for the reference markets (Greece, Turkey and Croatia) is that the customer expectations are already included in the pricing decisions of the market agents. The results obtained for the numbers of CCI that reach statistical significance (for four SEE countries) are really impressive despite the large amount of noise that characterizes the surveys. Here we can make a conclusion that the consumer sentiment information has influence on the capital market dynamics of Bulgaria, Macedonia, Slovenia, Romania, therefore on the prices of financial assets. Logically, we should make an assumption that the consumer expectations will have larger effect on the stocks of the companies especially dependent on consumption (e.g. consumer goods companies) than on the other stocks.

All things considered, we find evidence that consumer sentiment has predictive capability, connecting with the financial market dynamics of the emerging SEE capital markets. This conclusion is similar to the one proposed by Baumohl (2012) i.e the happiness of the consumers is important as when consumers feel less confident of the economy they tend not to be willing to make major purchases such as houses and cars which may derail the economic activity. Additionally, falling confidence is not favorable towards equities as it is an indication of declining business sales.

> **The impact of industrial sentiment on the capital market dynamics**

Table XI. Estimating results of GARCH models for the influence of the industrial confidence indicator on the stock market dynamics

Index	The most appropriate GARCH model	ICI (prob)
SOFIX	PGARCH (1,2) -t	6.15E-05 (0.9882)
CROBEX	PGARCH (2,1)-t	0.000679 (0.8019)
ACSP	EGARCH (2,1)-t	-0.000931 (0.8455)
MBI10	EGARCH (1,1)-t	0.000851 (0.2213)
BET	EGARCH (2,2)-t	0.000516 (0.7391)
SBITOP	EGARCH (1,2)-t	-1.32E-05 (0.9967)
BIST100	EGARCH (2,2)-t	0.001566 (0.4101)

Notes for Table XI.: The data of the industrial confidence indicator is included in the equation of EGARCH(p,q) or PGARCH(p,q) model.
Source: Author's calculations.

When we add the industrial confidence indicator (ICI) in the GARCH model equation, the results are quite different – none of the eight values of ICI is statistically significant at 5%.

Thus, there is not linkage between industrial sentiment and the market dynamics of the SEE capital markets. Actually, these results are not unexpected, in view of the assumption that business expectations do not affect the movement of the indices.

➤ The impact of inflation expectations on the capital market dynamics

Table XII. Estimating results of GARCH models for the influence of the inflation expectations on the stock market dynamics

Index	The most appropriate GARCH model	*InflExp (prob)*
SOFIX	*PGARCH(1,2) -t*	**0.060200 (0.0190)**
CROBEX	*PGARCH(2,1)-t*	**-0.000195 (0.0414)**
ACSP	*EGARCH(2,1)-t*	-0.000779 (0.5752)
MBI10	*EGARCH(1,1)-t*	**-0.007848 (0.0000)**
BET	*EGARCH(2,2)-t*	-0.004912 (0.3951)
SBITOP	*EGARCH(1,2)-t*	0.005638 (0.2260)
BIST100	*EGARCH(2,2)-t*	**0.010756 (0.0051)**
MONEX	*EGARCH(1, 2)-t*	-0.006195 (0.2610)

Notes for Table XII: The data of the inflation expectations is included in the equation of EGARCH (p,q) or PGARCH(p,q) model.
Source: Author's calculations.

The values of inflation expectations in the GARCH model equation are presented in Table XII. In macroeconomic theory the inflation expectations (InflExp) have a significant role in the formulation of the expectations-augmented Philips curve. In economics, the inflation expectations affect the overall production and through it indirectly influence financial market dynamics. Here we can make two important remarks. Firstly, statistically significant values of InflExp are registered for SEE indices – SOFIX (0.060200), CROBEX (-0.000195), MBI10 (-0.007848) and BIST100 (0.010756). Secondly, the absolute values of InflExp are in the range from 0.000195 (MBI10) to 0.060200 (SOFIX). Consequently, inflation expectations influence on the capital market dynamics of four SEE indices. Here we should note that the statistically significant values of inflation expectations are calculated for two reference financial markets –

Turkey and Croatia and two developing markets – Bulgaria and Macedonia. It's necessary to compare these results with the previous results revealing statistically significance of the CCI for Bulgarian and Macedonian indices. These conclusions are really remarkable because despite relatively illiquid trading on the markets and incomplete data surveys, the public expectations can be used for prediction purposes. Notably, inflation expectations are cointegrated with the real inflation and actually can be used to forecast it in the most of the examined countries.

To sum up, data for the inflation expectations have predictive power for the market performance of the stock indices, although relatively low values of InflExp (from 0.000195 to 0.060200).

Here, we can look at the macroeconomic fundamentals in order to evaluate the money supply influence on the stock market. What is more, money supply can have a negative impact on asset prices by its relationship to unexpected and future inflation. Keynesian hypothesis states that when money supply changes it will affect stock prices if it alters the expectations of future monetary policy. For instance, if the money supply increase, market participants will anticipate a contractionary monetary policy in the future which will lead to less investments and therefore increased interest rates. Thereby lowering stock market prices by a higher discount rate and lower expectations regarding future cash flows due to decreased economic activity (Sellin, 2001).

The emerging capital markets in Banja Luka, Sarajevo (Bosnia and Herzegovina), Bulgaria, Greece, Serbia, Macedonia, Romania and the reference Croatian market can be defined with inefficiency according to the EMH during the sample period. The indices ACSP (reference Greek capital market) and BIST100 (reference Turkish capital market) are with high values of their leverage coefficients indicating that market information has large effect on the volatility. Only Montenegrin stock exchange is market efficient due to the values of the coefficient of persistence and leverage effect. All things considered, it is reasonable to assume that SEE capital markets aren't efficient in the context of EMH. These results are consistent with the findings of Ivanov and et al. (Ivanov, I., Lomev, B., Bogdanova, B., 2012). They investigate the market efficiency of seven emerging East-European stock exchanges (Serbia, Romania, Turkey, Croatia, Russia, Ukraine, and Bulgaria) in respect of long-range dependence (LRD). The authors establish that for all of the examined indices there is clearly an indication for deviation from Random walk hypothesis and thus the studied markets manifest inefficiency.

The consumer sentiment information has influence on the capital market dynamics of Bulgaria, Macedonia, Slovenia, Romania, therefore on the prices of financial assets. Additionally, consumer expectations have predictive capability for the performance of the emerging SEE capital markets. In fact, these results are in agreement with results obtained by Gerunov (2014). Gerunov (2014) examines whether the stock market indices of twelve key EU economies are consistent with the implications of the Efficient Market Hypothesis (EMH) and if some publicly available information can be usefully utilized to forecast market movements. He finds enough evidence that the public expectations display predictive power for financial index dynamics in fully 6 (Germany, France, Poland, Bulgaria, Hungary and Greece) out of the 12 sampled countries. On the contrary, there is no linkage between industrial expectations and the dynamics of the SEE capital markets. Inflation expectations have impact on the performance of four SEE indices – Turkey, Croatia, Bulgaria and Macedonia. What is more, the inflation expectations information has predictive power for the market dynamics of the SEE stock exchanges. Our findings suggest that the public expectations impact the financial market dynamics in Bulgaria. Hence, macroeconomic indicators are important as they provide a tool for analyzing the current and future state of the Bulgarian economy. As the Bulgarian stock exchange is a concurrent part of our economy, indicators are used in order to evaluate stock market investments. Importantly, in Bulgarian emerging economy, the daily available source of information for households is the development of the financial market in Bulgaria. Generally, households in developing markets can only follow the economic outlook through the willingness to buy factor due to the fact that the level of income is close to subsistence.

> **Granger Causality Test for establishing the relationship between the returns of stock market indices and the public expectations**

Table XIII. Granger Causality Test for establishing the relationship between the returns of stock market indices and the public expectations *(2 lags)*

Country	Null hypothesis	F-Statistic	P value	Decision
Bulgaria	*CCI does not Granger Cause SOFIX* *SOFIX does not Granger Cause CCI**	1.23814 4.52609	0.2935 **0.0127**	*CCI ←SOFIX*
	ICI does not Granger Cause SOFIX *SOFIX does not Granger Cause ICI **	1.56678 6.67438	0.2129 **0.0018**	*ICI ←SOFIX*

	InflExp does not Granger Cause SOFIX	1.41943	0.2458	*Accept both hypotheses*
	SOFIX does not Granger Cause InflExp	0.22141	0.8017	
Croatia	*CCI does not Granger Cause CROBEX**	4.95546	**0.0086**	*CCI → CROBEX*
	CROBEX does not Granger Cause CCI	0.72313	0.4873	
	ICI does not Granger Cause CROBEX*	9.67617	**0.0002**	*ICI → CROBEX*
	CROBEX does not Granger Cause ICI	3.08037	0.0512	
	InflExp does not Granger Cause CROBEX	1.41724	0.2464	*Accept both hypotheses*
	CROBEX does not Granger Cause InflExp	0.26326	0.7690	
Greece	*CCI does not Granger Cause ACSP**	3.37128	**0.0375**	*CCI → ACSP*
	ACSP does not Granger Cause CCI	0.27428	0.7606	
	ICI does not Granger Cause ACSP*	6.43540	**0.0022**	*ICI → ACSP*
	ACSP does not Granger Cause ICI	1.69538	0.1878	
	InflExp does not Granger Cause ACSP	1.59078	0.2079	*InflExp ← ACSP*
	ACSP does not Granger Cause InflExp*	3.16488	**0.0457**	
Macedonia	*CCI does not Granger Cause MBI10*	0.37549	0.6897	*Accept both hypotheses*
	MBI10 does not Granger Cause CCI	0.49445	0.6141	
	ICI does not Granger Cause MBI10	1.60372	0.2073	*ICI ← MBI10*
	MBI10 does not Granger Cause ICI*	**3.97993**	**0.0224**	
	InflExp does not Granger Cause MBI10	0.35589	0.7031	*Accept both hypotheses*
	MBI10 does not Granger Cause InflExp	2.44835	0.1011	
Montenegro	*InflExp does not Granger Cause MONEX*	0.37747	0.6883	*Accept both hypotheses*
	MONEX does not Granger Cause InflExp	0.83245	0.4434	
Romania	*CCI does not Granger Cause BET*	2.22823	0.1120	*Accept both hypotheses*
	BET does not Granger Cause CCI	1.18324	0.3097	
	ICI does not Granger Cause BET	1.94334	0.1476	*ICI ← BET*
	BET does not Granger Cause ICI*	5.30432	**0.0062**	
	InflExp does not Granger Cause BET	0.46343	0.6302	*Accept both hypotheses*
	BET does not Granger Cause InflExp	2.38126	0.0967	
Slovenia	*CCI does not Granger Cause SBI TOP*	0.85898	0.4264	*CCI ← SBI TOP*
	SBI TOP does not Granger Cause CCI*	7.87640	**0.0006**	
	ICI does not Granger Cause SBI TOP	0.94945	0.3901	*ICI ← SBI TOP*
	SBI TOP does not Granger Cause ICI*	4.61392	**0.0119**	
	InflExp does not Granger Cause SBI TOP	0.95865	0.3866	*Accept both hypotheses*
	SBI TOP does not Granger Cause InflExp	2.69685	0.0719	
Turkey	*CCI does not Granger Cause BIST100*	2.68363	0.0735	*Accept both hypotheses*
	BIST100 does not Granger Cause CCI	0.18079	0.8349	
	ICI does not Granger Cause BIST100*	7.68700	**0.0008**	*ICI → BIST100*
	BIST100 does not Granger Cause ICI	0.37275	0.6898	
	InflExp does not Granger Cause BIST100	1.24282	0.2932	*Accept both hypotheses*
	BIST100 does not Granger Cause InflExp	2.13195	0.1242	

* *Null Hypothesis rejection at 5% significance level and acceptance of the Alternative Hypothesis which determine informational influence of the relevant variable*
Source: Authors' calculations.

Granger causality test is applied to test the relationship between capital market dynamics and public expectations - inflation expectations, consumer and business confidence. To determine the number of lags in our model, Akaike and Schwarz information criteria are applied. In our sample a lag of 2 is selected according to this criteria. The results of the test, presented in Table 4, show that there are interdependencies, both in the direction from public attitudes indicators to index returns and vice versa.

The results of the Granger Causality Test reveal that the hull hypothesis of no Granger causality from Consumer Confidence Indicator (CCI) to index return can be rejected at 5% significant level for two of the seven examined countries, namely Croatia and Greece. On the other hand, in Bulgaria and Slovenia, we prove that SOFIX and SBI TOP granger cause CCI. Therefore, only in the emerging capital markets of Bulgaria and Slovenia, index returns affect consumer expectations and attitudes. If we proceed from the assumptions of the Efficient Markets Hypothesis (EMH), the Greek and Croatian markets can be defined as efficient, which are also more developed than the Bulgarian and Slovenian markets.

Analyzing the results, we observe one way casual determining informational influence of stock market over the industrial confidence indicator (ICI) of the following countries: Bulgaria, Macedonia, Romania, Slovenia, leading to the conclusion that the hull hypothesis can be rejected. On the other hand, the relation "business confidence-capital market dynamics" is existed in the reference capital markets of Turkey, Greece and Croatia.

It is noteworthy that when there is a relation „business confidence - capital market", it refers only to the three reference capital markets. Consequently, we can define these markets as more developed than other markets considered. The raising degree of market completeness, related to the transmission mechanism of informational flows from industrial confidence to capital markets, may be accepted as an acknowledgment of EMH.

This would determine the capital markets of Turkey, Greece and Croatia as efficient according to the EMH. Additionally, we can consider the other financial markets as inefficient. To such a conclusion leads us the existing link "consumer confidence - capital market." Consumer confidence granger causes index return only in two of the reference capital markets - Greece and Croatia.

Due to the existing relation "capital market - business confidence" in the capital markets of Bulgaria, Macedonia, Romania, Slovenia we can assume that this is an indication for market inefficiency according to EMH, What is more, it could be considered as a prerequisite for strengthening the market trends. If EMH assumes that the flow of information is from the business environment to the market, i.e the public expectations and trust find their synthesized expression in market return, so the reversal of the direction of influence could strengthen the information impulses coming from the market. If business confidence follows up on the capital market dynamics, any positive market return would lead to the subsequent positive business expectations, increased confidence and further stimulate its participation in the capital market. This would lead to raised market activity of the business group and to strengthen the positive trend due to initial information coming from the market. However, this self-accelerating and self-sustaining market trend in the direction "capital market - business confidence" would also lead to a strengthening negative fluctuations of market returns. These results determine the capital markets of Bulgaria, Macedonia, Romania, Slovenia, except as less efficient according to the EMH, but also as predisposed to a more dynamic reflection of the impact of market impulses during the crisis periods.

Only in Greece - a country, considered by us as a reference one, we reveal that ACSP granger cause InflExp. In other words, the capital market dynamics of Greek market influence the inflation expectations.

> **The impact of sentiment indicators on the sovereign credit risk in Bulgaria**

The results by applying GARCH methodology for the influence of sentiment indicators on the Bulgarian capital market dynamic and sovereign credit risk are exposed in Table XIV.

Table XIV. Estimating results of GARCH models for the influence of the consumer confidence indicator on the capital market dynamics and credit default swap spreads of Bulgaria

Index	The most appropriate GARCH model	CCI (Prob)	InflExp (Prob)	ICI (Prob)	Index
SOFIX	PGARCH (1,2) -t	0.125358 (0.0113)	0.060200 (0.0190)	6.15E-05 (0.9882)	SOFIX
CDS	TGARCH (1,2)-t	0.251523 (0.0015)	0.046284 (0.0328)	0.023518 (0.0085)	CDS

Notes for Table XIV: The data of the inflation expectations and consumer confidence indicator is included in the equation of PGARCH(p,q) or TGARCH(p,q) model.
Source: Authors' calculations.

We can make a conclusion that the consumer sentiment information has influence on the capital market dynamics of Bulgaria, but remarkably, consumer confidence indicator registers significant high value (0.251523) in the equation of CDS spread. By this results, we prove that the happiness of the consumers is important not only for capital markets but for sovereign credit risk. The consumer confidence is an indicator which may predict and provoke a turmoil of economic activity. As it was proved, falling confidence is not favorable towards equities as it is an indication of declining business sales. Consequently, in the case of Bulgaria, consumer confidence should be considered as an economic indicator which derives most of its information content from past and current economic outlook. This is especially true during the financial crisis of 2008 when the future is uncertain and risky. InflExp is one of the main variables importance in predicting default risk. Inflation may be used as an indicator for economic stability. Aizenman el al. (2013) has explored the macoreconomic influence on sovereign and government default probability and his results reveals that inflation affects on CDS spreads variation. Comparing the influance of CCI, InflExp and ICI, it is important to report that all of the varibales are significant at 5% level. This confirms the hypothesis that sentiment indicators possesses a role of common or systematic risk factors of CDS spread changes. The significant results may be considered as a confirmation of the multiple-equilibria theory, namely that financial markets may take optimal behaviours sometimes during a period of turmoil and this leads to self-fulfilling liquidity crisis and self-fulfilling prophecies. These conclusions are proved by the bilateral relationship between Bulgarian capital market and CDS and CCI and CDS.

Granger causality test is applied to test the relationship between capital market dynamics and public expectations - inflation expectations, consumer and business confidence. On the other hand it is applied to reveal the relationship between public expectations and the public sector.

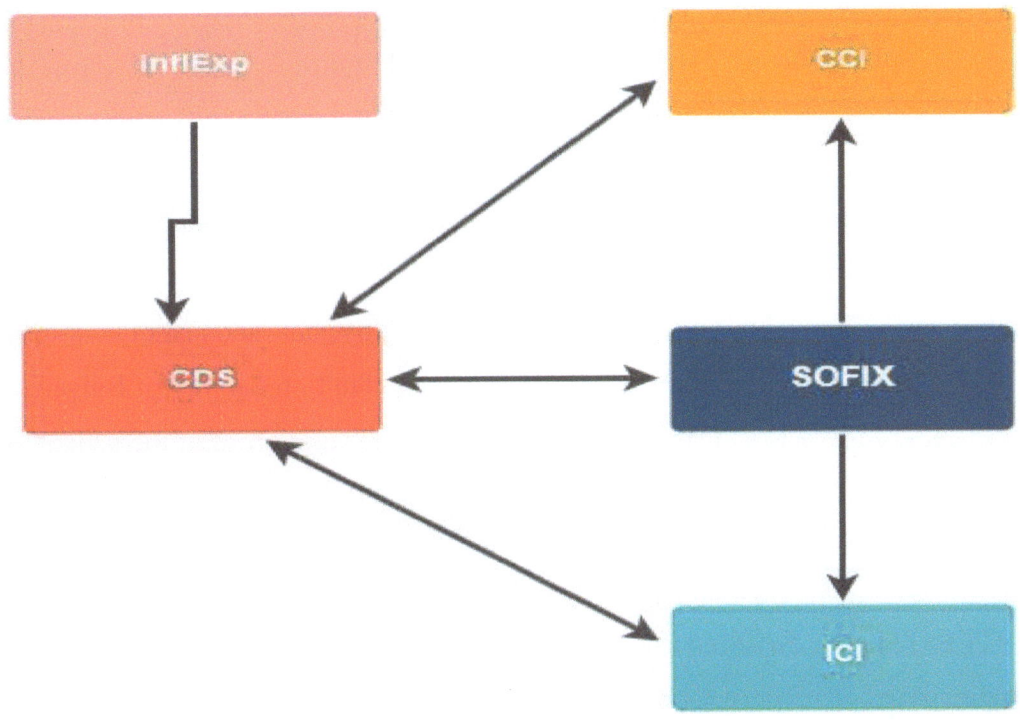

Graph 4: Significant Relations between Sentiment Indicators, Credit Default Swaps and Bulgarian Capital Market

> **Granger Causality Test for establishing the relationship between the returns of SOFIX, the public expectations and credit default swaps (CDS)**

Table XV. Granger Causality Test for establishing the relationship between the returns of SOFIX, the public expectations and credit default swaps (CDS) *(2 lags)*

Country	Null hypothesis	F-Statistic	P-value	Decision
BULGARIA	CCI does not Granger Cause SOFIX SOFIX does not Granger Cause CCI*	1.23814 **4.52609**	0.2935 **0.0127**	**CCI ←SOFIX**
	ICI does not Granger Cause SOFIX SOFIX does not Granger Cause ICI *	1.56678 **6.67438**	0.2129 **0.0018**	**ICI ←SOFIX**
	InflExp does not Granger Cause SOFIX SOFIX does not Granger Cause InflExp	1.41943 0.22141	0.2458 0.8017	**Accept both hypotheses**
	CDS does not Granger Cause SOFIX* SOFIX does not Granger Cause CDS*	**4.19547** **6.28103**	**0.0015** **0.0007**	**CDS →SOFIX** **CDS ←SOFIX**
	CCI does not Granger Cause CDS CDS does not Granger Cause CCI*	2.84151 3.01218	0.0135 0.0147	**CCI →CDS** **CDS ←CCI**
	InflExp does not Granger Cause CDS CDS does not Granger Cause InflExp	**5.07147** 1.26184	**0.0009** 0.2914	**InflExp →CDS**

| | ICI does not Granger Cause CDS | 4.31521 | 0.0215 | ICI → CDS |
| | CDS does not Granger Cause ICI* | 5.15026 | 0.0017 | CDS ← ICI |

Null Hypothesis rejection at 5% significance level and acceptance of the Alternative Hypothesis which determine informational influence of the relevant variable
Source: Authors' calculations.

Based on the results in Graph 4 and Table XIV, we may conclude that sentiment variables may explain CDS spread changes efficiently. We observe bilateral relations, which may be accepted as proves that turmoil periods may be led by panic and fear of investors without any enormous change in other factors. The increasing default probability of Bulgaria tends to lead to increase in investors' fear and panic. We accept this as a proof of the realization of the "snowball effect". The bilateral relationship between SOFIX and CDS reveals a transmission channel between "private sector" and "public sector".

CHAPTER THREE: Sovereign CDS Spread determinants and their impact on the competitiveness of the Bulgarian economy

3.1. Studies on sovereign CDS Spread determinants and their impact on the competitiveness of the economy

Understanding and defying determinants of credit spreads is vital for successful credit risk management by financial analysts, financial traders and economic policy makers. In the literature several methods which are focused on revealing determinants of credit default swap spreads are explored.

The structural approach, used by Merton (Merton, 1974)), Black and Cox (1976), Longstaff and Schwartz (1995) and Zhou (2001), has defined default as an increasing function of leverage. O'Kane and Turmball (Lehman Brothers, (2003)), today's structural models are based on Merton's invented in 1974. For default estimation, Merton has used asset value and asset volatility. According to structural approach default may be defined as a function of leverage, volatility, risk- free- rate and firm's assets.

On the other hand reduced form model defines default as an unexpected and unpredictable event. Jarrow and Turnbull (1995), Jarrow et al (1997) and Duffie and Singleton (1999) consider that default is the result of a random jump process without a specific reason for it. According to reduces form models, credit spread may be considered as a function of the following variables: probability of default, recovery rate and risk- free asset's yield.

Some researchers consider that both structural and reduced approaches have failed to fully reveal all the credit spread variations. (Dufresne and Goldstein (2001), Huang and Huang (2003).

In this research we examine the importance of country- specific and global factors in CDS pricing. We have found out that the global factors are indeed important. Nevertheless CDS is considered as an indicator of country's sovereign credit risk (OECD). Edwards (1984) has related country's probability of default to their sovereign credit spread by exploring macroeconomic determinants (Debt/ GNP; Reserves/ GNP; Investments/ GNP; Current account/ GNP; Growth and Inflation levels). In his study some of these country- specific determinants are considered as proxies for countries' ability to pay its debt. It exists several researches based on Edwards' research, namely Boehmer and Megginson (1990), Baeck et al. (2005), Dailami et al. (2008), Baldacci et al. (2011) and Beirne and Fratzeler (2013) – they have extended Edward's model by adding new macroeconomic determinants of sovereign CDS during different time periods by various econometric models. We have found out that country-specific fundamentals have substantial explanatory meaning, either.

A better understanding of the dynamics of sovereign credit spreads in debt crisis, which is explored in our research, is important because it is during the debt crisis that the sovereign credit spread is more concerned by the public (Blommestein, Eijffinger and Qian, 2015). Financial crises are preceded by periods in which investors avoid risk. Coudert and Gex (2006) test the possibility whether the main indexes for risk measurement are able to predict the occurrence of a crisis. They think that the "risk appetite" decreases before crisis. They still mark that the reverse reaction is possible. Crisis may be preceded by a period of strong "risk appetite" during which investors are too optimistic and in this way they create "speculative balloons" at prices of risk assets. The recent mortgage crisis started with the collapse of Bear Stearns is an example of such reaction. The results of their research state that indicators related to risk avoidance foresee the coming of crisis. That may explain the fact that in this paper we have included some variables which may be accepted as measurements of investors' behavior. The why the effect of these variables on sovereign CDS spreads is tested, is because of the more accurate determination in CDS variations. Fontana and Scheicher (2010) have already revealed the influence of investors' risk appetite on CDS variation. According to them the risk appetite variable should have negative influence on the credibility of CDS spreads as a sovereign risk indicator. According to Fontana and Scheicher (Fontana and Scheicher, 2010) the investors risk appetite influences the size of the CDS spreads, because it affects the demand of the CDS so an increasing investors' risk appetite means that they are more willing to bear their exposure to credit risk themselves. This means that they are less interested in insuring their risks and this leads to decreasing CDS spreads demand.

Pan and Singleton (2008) have explored the behavior and determinants of sovereign CDS in emerging markets and found out that CDS fluctuations may be caused by macroeconomic, political and financial market developments. They study SCDS in Turkey, Mexico and Korea and the results from their research reveals that CDS spreads are strongly connected to global risk determinants, rather than macroeconomic and country-specific variables.

Fontana and Scheicher (2010) have studied European sovereign CDS for the period from 2004 until 2010 as they have taken into account the financial crisis. Their main results have revealed that the increasing CDS pricing during the financial crisis is strong related to global risk aversion - a representative variable of global factors.

Longstaff et al. (2011) are the next authors who have studied the sovereign CDS determinants using country-specific and global variables for risk measurements. The results from his research confirm the Pan and Singleton's ones, namely the variables which have stronger influence on CDS spreads are the variables which represent systematic risk-global factors.

Applying a panel regression analysis for some developed economies Alper et al. (2012) have investigated determinants of CDS spread in order to reveal the pricing of sovereign credit risk. It has been found that over the period 2008-2010, country-specific financial determinants have a limited influence in the CDS spreads pricing. Global determinants are the main ones, used for predicting CDS spreads fluctuations.

3.2. Research methodology, Hypothesis and Data

We obesrve Bulgaria, because its national economies during the observed period, is characterized with high credit risk, high CDS spreads and increasing bankruptcy level. We use data with monthly frequencies, starting from March 2003 until June 2016. The dependent variable is CDS spread, denoted in Euro, obtained form Thomson Data Stream. Our model is based on the literature on credit risk. It is identified that both country- specific and global factors affect sovereign credit risk. Based on the aforementioned fact, we have used the following variables as explanatory variables:

➢ *Country- specific variables:*

- *Inflation* - it is one of the main variables importance in determing default risk. Inflation may be used as an indicator for economic stability, namely high levels of inflation indicate macroeconomic instability. Aizenman el al. (2013) has explored the macoreconomic influence on sovereign and government default probability and his results reveals that inflation affects on CDS spreads variation. The variable that we use for inflation is CPI (Consumer Price Index). It is obtained from Eurostat on a monthly basis. The expected sign of influence on CDS spread is positive because the higher inflation is, the higher default probability is.

- *Debt/ GDP* - Based on the approach of Gapen et al. (2005), we have used Debt as a ratio of GDP as a country- specific variable. According to Gapen's and numerous other researches Debt/ GDP is considered to be a leading factor into measuring country's default probability. Debt data is extracted from Eurostat on a quarterly basis so the variable is cubic spline interpolated in order to be turned into monthly numbers. The monthly data is expressed as a ratio to GDP. We expect the sign to be positive.

- *Current Account/GDP-* According to some policiy makers, ivestors and traders, current account balance's variations reflect country's economic situation. It may be used as an indicator about the ability of a country to repay its debt. Baldacci et al. (2008) has revealed that current account balance is a significant risk premium determinant. The variable is obtained from International Monetary Fund statistic and it is expressed as a ratio of GDP. The variable is cubic spline interpolated in order to receive monthly data. The expected sign is negative, because the higher current account suplus, the lower credit spread values.

- *Local capital markets* - Local capital markets may be considered as leading indicators of economic activity because they directly affect the wealth of economy. A well- functioning and developing capital markets may expand economic growth. (Kolstad, 2013). Longstaff et al. (2011) have revealed that local stock market returns may be accepted as a proxy for the conditions and the state of the local country economy.

➢ *Global Variables:*

- *The Risk- free rate* - The 3- month Euribor Eonia Spread- According to Merton's model (structural approach), default is determined by risk- free rate. Risk- free rate, firm growth and the default probability are in a strong relationship. Increasing both variables- the risk- free rate and the firm growth- leads to reduction of the default probability. We have included risk- free rate as a credit default swap spread determinant not only because of stuctural approach, but because of Fontana and Scheicher's (2010) research results. They explore its influence in highly distressed countries in Europe- just the same as ours- Bulgaria, Romania, Portugal, Italy, Ireland, Greece and Spain. The 3- month Euribor Eonia Spread is used to proxy the risk- free rate in Europe. It may be used as an indicator for both credit risk and market liquidity. The Euro Inter Bank Offered Rate is the rate at which major European banks borrow funds from each other with maturity from one week to twelve months. The Euro OverNight Index represents the one- day interbank interest rate for the Eurozone. We use the difference between the 3- month Euribor and the three month Eonia rate as a measure for risk- free rate. The expected sign is negative because the higher interest rates, the lower credit spreads . In the equation of the linear regression we call this variable eureon.

- *The US economy - PMI index* - After the last financial crisis, the fact that the US economy may be considered as a „reflection" of the world economy, has increased its significance. Breitenfeller and Wagner (2012) have explored iTraxx Euro area and have found out that global economy and corporate CDS spreads are strongly correlated. The proxy of the state of the US economy, the PMI (Purchasing Managers' Index) index is included in our research. PMI is an index developed from monthly business surveys, used to monitor the conditions of industries and business. Investors use PMI as a leading indicator for economic health. It is extremely important for international investors, which reflects economic growth. PMI enables invetors and decision- makers to improve the efficiency of their investments and business plan. Data on PMI is obtained is obtained from ISM reports on a monthly basis. The expected sign in the regression is negative.

- *The Euro- area economy - EuroStoxx50-* This global variable is used as a proxy for the state of the Euro- area economy. Including this global variable into our research, we try to establish and capture international spillover effects (Dieckman and Plank, 2011). In a monetary union, a country's default probability may be affected by the willingness of the other member counties to bail out. In this case, a decline in the union wide economy, proxy by the EuroStoxx50 will increase SCDS. So, the expected sign is negative.

- *Volatility- VDAX Volatility Index-* Based on the structural approach, volatility is one of the main determinants in coutry's default risk. It may be used as an indicator of investors' risk appetite. The VDAX Volatility Index is selected as a measure for the Risk Appetite. This index is analogous to the VIX. It represents the changes in the risk aversions of investors. The data is obtained from Deutsche Burse in monthly basis. The expected sign is negative, either.

- *Investors expectations-* The varables that we use for investors' expectations and assessments are ESI (Economic Sentiment Indicator) and ZEW Economic Sentiment. ZEW Economic Sentiment Indicator is an indicator which reflects the amalgamation of the sentiment of 350 economists regarding the economic climate in Europe for the next six months. Economic Sentiment Indicators combines assessments and expectations coming from business and cosumer surveys for different sectors:Industry, consumers, construction and retail. The data of the both variables are in monthly basis and the expected signs are negative, the more optimistic are the investors about future economic climate in Europe, the lower are credit default spreads.

Table XVI. Expected signs of the explanatory variable into determining the dependent variable CDS

	Variables:	Expected sign:
Country-specific variables:	CPI	Positive +
	Debt/ GDP	Positive +
	CA/ GDP	Negative -
	LSMI	Negative -
Global variables:	Risk- free rate	Negative -
	VDAX	Negative -
	ZEW	Negative -
	ESI	Negative -
	PMI	Negative -
	EuroStoxx50	Negative -

Source: Authors' classification based on previous researches.

➤ **Cubic Spline Interpolation**

Because of the fact that some of the researched variables are available on quarterly basis, we use cubic spline interpolation to convert them into monthly data basis. A cubic spline is a segmented function consisting of third- degree polynomical functions joined together making the whole curve and its first and second derivative continuous. Many researchers prefer cubic spline interpolation to linear interpolation (Kolstad, 2013).

➤ **Unit Root Test**

Before proceeding to the election of the econometric method, it is necessary to establish stationarity for all of the explored variables: dependent- CDS spreads- and explanatory variables. One of the used panel unit root tests is the test, developed by Levin, Lin and Chu (2002). The null hypothesis means that Ho: each time series contains a unit root, against the alternative hypothesis H1 : each time series is stationary. The test procedure includes four steps.

> **Oridnary Least Squares Regression**

For the establishment of credit default spreads determinants, we use linear regression. The study is based on evaluating linear regression equation by means of the method of least squared (OLS regression- ordinary least squares regression) and it is included in the dummy variable equation- dummy variable. Using a dummy variable is intended to divide the regression equation of two sub-periods- Euro zone memberhip and being not a member of the Euro zone. To conduct calculation the dummy variable takes two values- (0) being not members of the Euro zone and (1) if Bulgaria and Romania become members of the Euro zone.

To determine Credit Default Spreads, using OLS- method, we apply an econometric equation with the following standard form:

$$CDS_{it} = \alpha + \beta_1 CPI_{it} + \beta_2 Debt/GDP_{it} + \beta_3 CA/GDP_{it} + \beta_4 LCMI_{it} + \beta_5 (Euro\ zone\ 1/0) + \varepsilon_{it} \quad (10)$$

$$CDS_{it} = \alpha + \beta_1 eureon_{it} + \beta_2 VDAX_{it} + \beta_3 ZEW_{it} + \beta_4 ESI_{it} + \beta_5 PMI_{it} + \beta_5 EuroStoxx50_{it} + \beta_6 (Euro\ zone\ 1/0) + \varepsilon_{it} \quad (11)$$

Where:

CDS_{it} - Dependent variable- Credit default swap of the i- th country at time period t, explained by country- specific variables in equation (10) and by global variables in equation (11).

3.3. Research results and Discussion

Before proceeding to the regression models, we have applied panel unit root test. Table XVII shows the results of the Levin, Lin and Chu test (2002) for all researched variables. The results indicate that for all of the panel time series level data are not stationary so we have to transform them into first difference. According to the results in table XVII the first differences of the time series are stationary. The right column shows the test results for the first difference of the time series used in the regression analysis. A large negative t- statistic and the high significance level indicate the rejection of the null hypothesis and therefore, stationarity of the time series. Because of the fact that the first differences of the time series are stationary, we may conclude that they are integrated in order one.

Table XVII. Panel Unit Root Test Results

Variable:	1-st difference statistic:	p-value:
CDS spreads	-17.7356	0.0000
CPI	-11.1261	0.0000
CA/ GDP	-34.2120	0.0000
Debt/ GDP	-12.7092	0.0000
SOFIX	-17.6166	0.0000
Risk- free rate (eureon)	-5.48419	0.0000
VDAX	-21.5523	0.0000
ZEW	-10.2279	0.0000
ESI	-7.61886	0.0000
PMI	-6.53913	0.0000
EuroStoxx50	-10.7502	0.0000

Note: All of the variables are stationary at first difference.
Source: Authors' calculations.

For the estimation of the first diiference of the explored variables, we use the following equation:

$$FirstDiff = \frac{VarValue_{it}}{VarValue_{it-1}} \qquad (12)$$

Where:

FirstDiff - the first difference of the explored variable;

$VarValue_{it}$ - the value of the explored variables for the i- th country at moment t;

$VarValue_{it-1}$ - the value of the explored variable for the i- th country at the moment t-1.

> **OLS' results from CDS country specific determinants:**

Table XVIII. Country- specific determinants of CDS spreads (Dependent variable CDS spreads).

Variable:	Expected sign:	Coefficient:	t- statistic:	p-value:
C		0.299737	2.184903	0.0034
CA/ GDP	Negative	-0.267710	-0.722512	0.4702
LCMI	Negative	-0.482177	-23.91985	0.0006
Euro zone=1		-2.855384	-3.488286	0.0071
CPI	Positive	0.912364	0.410023	0.6819
Debt	Positive	2.792615	9.009798	0.0295
R- squared	0.454550			
Adjusted R- squared:	0.450676			

Source: Author's calculation.

The results of linear regression, including country specific variables and the dummy variable Euro zone=1 for the explored time period, has revealed their strong influence to CDS spreads. To confirm these findings, we first consider the value of R^2 as an indicator, stating how much of the variability of CDS spreads may be explained by the regression equation. The explanatory variables, as evidenced according to the results in table XVIII, are able to account for the 45.45% of the variation of CDS spreads, which means that country- specific variables are significant factors in determining sovereign credit spreads for the explored seven countries. Equally important as the fact that the variables do indeed influence the CDS spreads is whether or not coefficients of the variables have the correct sign base on what is expected in theory. All of the four explored variables in equation (10) have the correct signs. These results are conconfirm the ones of Edwards (1984), Boehmer and Megginson (1990), Beck et al. (2005), Dailami et al. (2008), Baldacci et al. (2011) and Beirne and Fratzeler (2013) which conclude that macroeconomic conditions of a national economy are significant variables in CDS dynamics.

Firstly, the results of linear regression, including country specific variables and the dummy variable Euro zone=1 reveals statistical significance of the dummy variable and its value is (-2.855384). It has been established that the negative sign and symbol of Euro zone=1 leads to reduction in the regression constant C, whose coefficient in the regression equation is (0.299737).

Secondly, local capital market index, euro zone= 1 dummy variable and debt- all have a statistically significant effect on CDS spreads. All of these variables reflect the sovereign credit default swaps spreads and have the expected sign. But we should consider the fact that if a country's debt increases its level, it will lead to significant effects on CDS spreads (in order to expand them). According to the results in the linear regression equation, the significant effect of country' indebtness may be neutralized by higher market capitalization, market development and membership in the Euro zone.

In table XIX, we have revealed the results from the OLS equation, but in this case dummy variable Euro zone is equal to zero (Euro zone= 0). The established value of Euro zone= 0 is positive and statistically significant with a coefficient value equal to (2.855384), and the coefficient value of the constant C is negative (-0.691486). We should take into account that according to the results in table XVIII and table XIX, opposite results are observed. From this, we can draw conclusions opposite to those characteristic of a country Euro zone member, and namely, if Bulgaria and Romania become

Euro zone members, they will decrease their credit default spreads because now not being members leads to CDS spreads growth.

Table XIX. Country- specific determinants of CDS spreads (dependent variable CDS spreads)

Variable	Expected sign	Coefficient	t- statistic	p-value
C		-0.691486	-2.625782	0.0042
CA/ GDP	Negative	-0.267710	-0.722512	0.4702
LCMI	Negative	-0.482177	-23.91985	0.0006
Euro zone=0		2.855384	3.488286	0.0071
CPI	Positive	0.912364	0.410023	0.6819
Debt	Positive	2.792615	9.009798	0.0295
R- squared	0.454550			
Adjusted R- squared:	0.450676			
AIC	9.251272			
SIC	9.289851			

Source: Author's calculation

> **OLS' results from CDS global and behavioral determinants:**

To reveal the influence of global and behavioral variables into CDS spreads, we have used linear regression equation (11). The results are shown in table XX:

Table XX. Global determinants of CDS spreads (Dependent variable CDS spreads)

Variable	Expected sign	Coefficient	t- statistic	p-value
C		-0.700295	-2.305536	0.0041
Risk- free rate	Negative	-2.480249	-0.279850	0.7797
PMI	Negative	1.237054	1.565636	0.1180
Euro zone=1		9.917045	3.204949	0.0014
VDAX	Negative	-1.550437	-4.754940	0.0000
ESI	Negative	-1.467598	-2.207381	0.0277
ZEW	Negative	-0.071276	-0.464329	0.6426
EuroStoxx50	Negative	-2.491003	-2.003597	0.0488
R- squared	0.748007			
Adjusted R- squared	0.630010			
AIC	5.02971			
SIC	4.09179			

Source: Author's calculation

The results of linear regression, including global variables and the dummy variable Euro zone=1 for the explored time period, has revealed really significant influence to CDS spreads. To confirm these findings, we consider the value of R^2 as an indicator, stating how much of the variability of CDS spreads may be explained by the regression equation. In this second model, the explanatory variables, as evidenced according to the results in Table XX , are able to account for the 74.80% of the variation of CDS spreads, which means that global variables are strong significant factors in determining sovereign credit spreads for the explored seven countries. In direct comparison of the model (1) and model (2)- country- specific and global determinants of CDS spreads, we may come to the conclusion that the latter demonstrates better results from the application of the regression evaluation of determination of sovereign credit default swap spreads. This statement is confirmed by the R- squared values, the values of the test statistics associated with the Akaike and Schwartz criteria (Akaike info criterion and Schwarz criterion). As evidenced by the results of equation (11), the improvement of the explanatory power is substantial- 74.80% of the variability of CDS spreads is explained by the regression model compared to 45.45% for the equation (10). These results are consistent with the results of Pan and Singleton (2008), Fontana and Scheicher (2010), Longstaff et al. (2011) and Alper et al. (2012), which mean that CDS spreads are strongly connected to global risk determinants, rather than macroeconomic and country-specific variables. Analyzing data from the two models we cannot fail to note that the values of the Std. Error, t- Statistic, P- value, Probability, the coefficients of the regression equations are statistically significant and different from zero. Thus, we can determine that the models, expressed by equation (10) and equation (11) provide valuable insights about credit default spreads determinants and the role of the Euro zone membership.

The significant variables in equation (11) are the dummy variable, Eurostoxx50 and VDAX and ESI. All of them have the correct expected sign in the equation. The risk- appetite, measured by VDAX, has the correct sign, either. Regression results reveal that increasing risk appetite has a decreasing impact on sovereign CDS spreads, which is in support of Fontana and Scheicher's (2010) results. The effects of ESI and ZEW sentiment indicators are less strong and negative than the influence of VDAX into CDS spreads so by equation (11), we have found that the explored behavioral variables have been related to credit risk spreads. EuroStoxx50 is a variable which indicates significance in the regression equation. The expected sign is negative and its value is (- 2.491003). This confirms Dieckman and Plank's (2011) results, namely decline in EuroStoxx50 will increase sovereign credit default swap spreads because a country's default probability may be strongly related to the conditions of other member countries.

On the other hand we should mention that the risk- free- rate is not significant. It may due to the fact that during the explored time period- 2003-2016- the effects of Euribor on the CDS spreads has been limited, as central banks have used monetary policy to counteract the effects of the financial and sovereign debt crisis.

The sign of the dummy variable Euro zone= 1 is positive with a value (9.917045) and the value of the regression coefficient C is (-0.700295). According to these results and the variables used in equation (11), we may conclude that systematic risk has better explanatory value in CDS spreads determination. In conditions of systematic risk influence, the Euro zone membership leads to increase in CDS spreads. This means that being members of the Euro zone, countries will be strongly affected by the systematic risk and contagion effects.

When we change the value of the dummy variable in equation (11), we observe opposite results again. This means that the value of the Euro zone (-9.917045) leads to reduction in C coefficient' Value (9.126750). So, we may conclude that for Bulgaria and Romania- not being members of the Euro zone- reduces their CDS spreads in a way that neutralize the effects of the others statistical significant variables- VDAX with coefficient value (- 1.550437), ZEW- (- 0.071276) and EuroStoxx 50- (- 2.491003).

Table XXI. CDS spreads (Dependent variable CDS spreads)

Variable:	Expected sign:	Coefficient:	t- statistic:	p-value:
C		9.216750	4.406220	0.0000
Risk- free rate	Negative	-2.480249	-0.279850	0.7797
PMI	Negative	1.237054	1.565636	0.1180
Euro zone=0		-9.917045	-3.204949	0.0014
VDAX	Negative	-1.550437	-4.754940	0.0000
ESI	Negative	-1.467598	-2.207381	0.0277
ZEW	Negative	-0.071276	-0.464329	0.6426
EuroStoxx50	Negative	-2.491003	-2.003597	0.0488
R- squared	0.748007			
Adjusted R- squared:	0.630010			
AIC	5.02971			
SIC	4.09179			

Source: Authors' calculation.

According to the aforementioned results, we may conclude that the model, which examines the global and behavioral credit default swap determinants, has a better explanation in CDS spreads variation. This statement is proved by the R- squared value and the values of the test statistics associated with the Akaike and Schwartz criteria (Akaike info criterion and Schwarz criterion). The other fact that we should mention is the key role of Euro zone membership in CDS spreads determining. It possesses opposite effects in both equations (10) and (11). When we explore, country-specific determinants influence (equation (10)), Euro zone membership neutralizes the effects of the debt level and local capital markets and reduces CDS spreads. It has the following effects in equation (11) - when exploring global variables effects- in these cases when the country is not an Euro zone member, global determinants are neutralized by the value of the Euro zone membership's coefficient.

This chapter examines the determinants of CDS spreads and the potential influence on the competitiveness and efficiency of the Bulgarian and Romanian national economies. One of the main contributions of this research is that in addition to variables that proxy for global and macroeconomic CDS spreads determinants, we also employ variables that proxy for behavioral determinants. Another contribution of the paper is that at our knowledge, this is the first paper that examines the relationship between being Eurozone membership influence and derivative market. *Fluctuations of global financial and behavioral variables dominate in explaining CDS pricing change so, it means that systematic risk has stronger influence in CDS pricing than the individual risk in Bulgaria.* In conditions of systematic risk influence, the Euro zone membership leads to increase in CDS spreads. This means that being members of the Euro zone, countries will be strongly affected by the systematic risk and contagion effects. When we explore, macroeconomic determinants influence, the Euro zone membership neutralizes the effects of the debt level and local capital markets and reduces CDS spreads. When exploring global variables effects- in these cases when the country is not a Euro zone member, global determinants are neutralized by the value of the Euro zone membership's coefficient. The country- specific variables, such as inflation, debt/GDP, current account/ GDP, local capital markets' indexes – have an explanatory power, either but it is less strong than the explanatory power of the global determinants. We also report evidence that sentiment may play role in CDS spread determination, along with other facts, but they are not significant in determining the Euro zone membership probability. These results confirm the ones of Fontana and Scheicher's (2010). This analysis suggests that the traditional measures (Merton's model) of sovereign default risk are not sufficient to measure it. The research can provide an interesting starting point for future research on sovereign CDS spreads. There are various other aspects that can be explored. For one, it might be valuable to see what the impact of the respective variables tested for this research is in different time periods: pre- crisis, crisis and post- crisis period. It is very well possible that the selected explanatory variables are able to explain the CDS spreads in different manner dependent on the time period.

CHAPTER FOUR: Relationship between Bulgarian sovereign credit risk and accounting information

4.1. Studies on the relationship between Bulgarian sovereign credit risk and accounting information

Understanding and defying determinants of credit spreads is vital for successful credit risk management by financial analysts, financial traders and economic policy makers. In the literature several methods which are focused on revealing determinants of credit default swap spreads are explored. We accept CDS as a financial instrument which is appropriate for effective management with credit risk. It exists researches that reveal that equity markets lead the CDS one in credit price discovery (Noreden and Weber, 2004; Pena and Forte, 2009; Forte and Lovreta, 2009). On the other hand accounting data and their relationship with equity market is explored. In their research Ball and Brown (1968) examine whether stock prices respond to the news of financial statements. They conclude that markets react to information content provided by accounting data and it is useful for investors. Beaver, Clarke and Wright (1979) prove that accounting data is an important informational source for equity investors. Their findings are in line with the Capital Asset Pricing Model (CAPM), namely: the greater abnormal return, the stronger stock price reaction. Another approach tries to explain the relationship between accounting data and its ability to predict default and bankruptcies (Altman, 1968; Ohlosn, 1980; Hillegeist et al., 2002). Demirovic and Thomas (2007) reveal that accounting measures are important instruments for measuring credit risk variance. Duffie and Lando (2001) explore a model, by which they apply accounting information as a determinant in credit risk pricing. Their results are supported by the research results of Callen, Livnat and Segal (2009) and Das, Hanouna and Sarin (2009). They prove that accounting data has a significant role in CDS pricing and the determine CDS premiums as measurements for credit risk.

Exploring the relationship between accounting area and CDS spreads is a topic which is gaining more attention. Chakravarty (2010) proves that CDS prices are in a negative correlation with the optional accounting conservatism.

The literature proposes three approaches which explain pricing of credit risk: Structural approach used by Merton (Merton, 1974; Black and Cox, 1976; Longstaff and Schwartz, 1995 and

Zhou, 2001); reduced approach (Jarrow and Turnbull, 1995; Jarrow et al., 1997 and Duffie and Singleton, 1999) and a Hybrid approach.

Callen, Livnat and Segal (2009) determine accounting information in the hybrid model as a quiet abstract because of the lack of specific accounting variables in the Duffie and Lando's model. However, Duffie and Lando conclude that their approach may be extended to accommodate other variables for accounting information. The hybrid model determines accounting information transparency: earnings, cash flows as determinants of CDS pricing. Yu (2002) and Duffie and Lando (2001) reveal that accounting information is a relevant informational source for holders debt capital.

The regression approach of Collin- Dufresne et al. (2001) tries to identify theoretical determinants of credit risk, either. It estimates bond yield spread by independent variables which measure corporate credit spread. Aunon- Nerin et al. (2002), Benkert (2004), Abid and Naifar (2006), Ericsson el al. (2009), Batta (2002) and Das et al. (2009) investigate pricing CDS premium by a regression approach, either. Benkert (2004) explores CDS pricing process by the following variables: earnings to sales, earnings to interest, leverage and volatility. He exposes that earning variables possess positive influence on CDS premiums.

4.2. Reaserch Methodology and data

In this chapter, we analyze the relation between accounting information and sovereign CDS in Bulgaria. We use data with quarterly frequency. The examined period is from 1st January 2009 to 31th December 2016.

- *CDS spreads*- sovereign credit default swap (CDS) spread is a variable denoted in Euro, obtained from Thomson Data Stream. After the financial crisis of 2007, it has been revealed the importance of debt markets for functioning of the financial system and the financing of public corporations. CDS spreads resemble to insurance premiums and it reflects market perception about risk of default or other „credit event" related ro reference entity (Flannery, 2010). That is the main reason for choosing sovereign CDS within debt markets. In this paper we focus on the sovereign credit default swap market. In the case of sovereign CDS, the country's credit risk should be transferred between CDS buyers and CDS sellers. During the financial crisis and the sovereign debt crisis, many European countries have been under pressure to raise funds to finance fast growing fiscal deficits, so this provoked many investors to insure against losses on holding sovereign debt.

- *Risk- free rate* - According to Merton's model (structural approach), default is determined by risk- free rate. Risk- free rate, firm growth and the default probability are in a strong relationship. Increasing both variables- the risk- free rate and the firm growth- leads to reduction of the default probability. We have included risk- free rate as a credit default swap spread determinant not only because of stuctural approach, but because of Fontana and Scheicher's (2010) research results. They explore its influence in highly distressed countries in Europe- just the same as ours- Bulgaria, Romania, Portugal, Italy, Ireland, Greece and Spain. We include risk- free rate as a control variable i.e. to regulate for time clustering in the data. Our regression model follows the one of Das et al. (2009). The risk- free rate is included as a proxy for macroeconomic environment. We apply 3 month Euribor rate as an indicator for risk- free rate. The Euro Inter Bank Offered Rate is the rate at which major European banks borrow funds from each other with maturity from one week to twelve months. The 3- month Euribor data is obtained from the database of the European Central Bank.

> ### *Accounting variables*

We use accounting variables for firm size, profitability, leverage, liquidity, asset utilization, consecutive losses and current asset utilization. Ratios and measures were chosen on the basis of their popularity in assessing credit worthiness in prior literature and on the availability of data. The accounting information was taken from the financial reports of the examined firms. Additionally, Bulgarian capital market requires its listed issuers to disclose detailed quarterly financial reports. Thus, all accounting data was acquired from the website of the Bulgarian stock exchange (BSE). Using the accounting information from the financial reports we calculate the following variables for each of the twenty analyzed Bulgarian companies:

- *Firm size*–it is the natural logarithm of the value of total assets. What is more, Vassalou and Xing (2004) note that firm size is an important factor in the determination of a company's credit risk.

- *Leverage* – firms' leverage is measured as total liabilities divided by total assets. Basing on Merton's model (1974), we imply that leverage ratio is one of the main determinants of the probability of default. According to Shumway (2001), leverage is one of the variables that has been revealed to assure for financial distress to stock returns and volatilities. Logically, a higher value of leverage coefficient leads to an increased level of credit risk. Consequently, we expect that increased levels of leverage will be associated negatively with the CDS spreads. The more levered the firm, the higher probability of default.

- *Liquidity* – we use the cash-to-assets ratio and current ratio to estimate the liquidity of the sample companies. The cash-to-assets ratio is the current value of marketable securities and cash, divided by the current liabilities. On the other hand, the current ratio is measured as current liabilities divided by current assets. Here, again, it is expected that liquidity has a negative coefficient in the OLS regression.

- *Profitability* – we calculate ROA (return on assets) and EBIT-margin (Earnings before interests and taxes divided by sales). The formula for the ROA is the following: Earnings / total assets. Das et al. (2009) establish that return on assets is a statistically significant factor in the fluctuation in CDS spreads. Increase in profitability of a corporation should lead to reduction its credit risk, because of the fact that the increased profitability, the entity is wealthier and probability of default reduces its level.

- *Asset utilization* (SalesAssets) is calculated by dividing sales by total assets. Altman (1968) finds that SalesAssets ratio is a very good measure in the valuation of bankruptcy probability combining with other accounting ratios.

- *Consecutive losses* – According to Ohlosn (1980), consecutive losses are measured as a dummy variable that receives the value one if net income was negative for the last two quarters and zero otherwise. James Ohlosn (1980) is acknowledged to be the first researcher to conduct a comprehensive study of bankruptcy using logit analysis.

- *Current asset utilization* (SalesCurrent) is measured as sales divided by current assets. This ratio is supposed to have a negative effect on the CDS spreads.

Table XXII: Independent variables and their expected signs

	Variables	*Expected sign*
Accounting Variables:	Lnsize	Negative -
	Leverage	Positive +
	Cash	Negative -
	Current	Negative -
	ROA	Negative -
	EBIT	Negative -
	SalesAssets	Negative -
	INTWO	Positive +

	SalesCurrent	Negative -
Control Variable	Risk- free rate	Positive +

Source: Authors' classification based on previous researches
Sample companies

Table XXII summarizes the explanatory variables used in the regressions and displays the expected sign for the coefficients as well the type of data that is used.

We analyze 20 separate corporate entities from various industries in Bulgaria. All of the companies included in the sample are public firms that listed their common shares on the Bulgarian stock exchange (BSE). Additionally, stock indices SOFIX and BGBX40 are based on the market capitalization of the issues of common shares of the selected Bulgarian companies.

SOFIX constituents must meet certain minimum criteria for liquidity, market capitalization, free-float and number of shareholders. We examine firms from different sectors - for example: manufacturing, financial and insurance activities; accommodation and food service activities. Here we have to make two remarks. First, we have chosen exactly these twenty firms because all of the necessary accounting information is available for the whole examined post-crisis period that is from 2009 to 2016. Second, the analyzed companies are public ones and BSE requires its listed issuers to disclose detailed quarterly financial reports. What is more, the accounting data was collected and processed as of 15.08.2017.

Table XXIII. Sample companies

Company name	Sector	Subsector	Stock index
Sopharma AD-Sofia	Manufacturing	Manufacture of basic pharmaceutical products and pharmaceutical preparations	SOFIX, BGBX40
Neochim AD-Dimitrovgrad	Manufacturing	Manufacture of chemicals and chemical products	SOFIX, BGBX40
EuroholdBulgaria AD-Sofia	Financial and insurance activities	Financial service activities, except insurance and pension funding	SOFIX, BGBX40
Industrial Capital Holding AD-Sofia	Financial and insurance activities	Financial service activities, except insurance and pension funding	SOFIX, BGBX40
BulgarianRealEstateFund REIT-Sofia	Financial and insurance activities	Financial service activities, except insurance and pension funding	SOFIX, BGBX40
Monbat AD-Sofia	Manufacturing	Manufacture of electrical equipment	SOFIX, BGBX40

M+S Hydraulic AD-Kazanlak	Manufacturing	Manufacture of machinery and equipment n.e.c.	SOFIX, BGBX40
StaraPlaninaHold AD-Sofia	Financial and insurance activities	Financial service activities, except insurance and pension funding	SOFIX, BGBX40
Advance Terrafund REIT-Sofia	Financial and insurance activities	Financial service activities, except insurance and pension funding	SOFIX, BGBX40
Albena AD-Albena	Accommodation and food service activities	Food and beverage service activities	SOFIX, BGBX40
Chimimport AD-Sofia	Financial and insurance activities	Financial service activities, except insurance and pension funding	SOFIX, BGBX40
Holding Varna AD-Varna	Financial and insurance activities	Financial service activities, except insurance and pension funding	SOFIX, BGBX40
Alcomet AD-Shumen	Manufacturing	Manufacture of basic metals	SOFIX, BGBX40
Sopharma Properties REIT-Sofia	Financial and insurance activities	Financial service activities, except insurance and pension funding	BGBX40
YuriGagarin PLC-Plovdiv	Manufacturing	Printing of reproduction of recorded media	BGBX40
Billboard AD-Sofia	Manufacturing	Printing of reproduction of recorded media	BGBX40
HydraulicElementsand Systems AD-Yambol	Manufacturing	Manufacture of machinery and equipment n.e.c.	BGBX40
Industrial Holding Bulgaria PLC-Sofia	Financial and insurance activities	Financial service activities, except insurance and pension funding	BGBX40
ElhimIskra AD-Pazardzhik	Manufacturing	Manufacture of electrical equipment	BGBX40
Aktiv Properties REIT-Plovdiv	Financial and insurance activities	Financial service activities, except insurance and pension funding	BGBX40

Source: Authors' calculations

Notes: Table 1 displays all companies included in the sample and also the specific sector/subsector and the stock index which is based on the market capitalization of the issues of common shares of the examined firms (to 15.08.2017).

The table displays all companies included in the sample. Also, the specific sector and subsector of all examined firms are presented.

> ### *Panel Unit Root Test: Summary*

The recent literature suggests that panel-based unit root tests have higher power than unit roots tests based on individual time series. We describe the panel unit root test by the following equation:

$$y_t = p_i y_{it-1} + x_{it}\delta_i + \varepsilon_{it} \tag{13}$$

Where i=1,2...N cross-section units, which are observed over periods t=1.2...T_i; x_{it}- exogenous variables, including fixed effects or individual trends; p_i- autoregressive coefficient; ε_{it}- errors, which are assumed to be mututally independent idiosyncratic disturbance.

We may conclude that:

1. If : p_i :< 1, y_i is considered to be trend stationary;
2. If : p_i := 1, then y_i contains a unit root. The null hypothesis assumes a common unit root process.

> ***Vector Autoregressions (VARs)***

The vector autoregression (VAR) is commonly used for forecasting systems of interrelated time series and for analyzing the dynamic impact of random disturbances on the system of variables. The VAR approach sidesteps the need for structural modeling by treating every endogenous variable in the system as a function of the lagged values of all of the endogenous variables in the system.

The mathematical representation of a VAR is the following equation:

$$y_t = A_1 y_{t-1} + ... + A_p y_{t-p} + Bx_t + \varepsilon_t \tag{14}$$

where y_t is a k vector of endogenous variables, x_t is a d vector of exogenous variables, $A_1,...,A_p$ and B are matrices of coefficients to be estimated, and ε_t is a vector of innovations that may be contemporaneously correlated but are uncorrelated with their own lagged values and uncorrelated with all of the right-hand side variables.

Since only lagged values of the endogenous variables appear on the right-hand side of the equations, simultaneity is not an issue and OLS yields consistent estimates. Moreover, even though the innovations ε_t may be contemporaneously correlated, OLS is efficient and equivalent to GLS since all equations have identical regressors.

> ***Granger Causality in VAR***

The VAR can be considered as a means of conducting causality tests, or more specifically Granger causality tests. Granger causality really implies a correlation between the current value of one variable and the past values of others, it does not mean changes in one variable cause changes in another. By using a F-test to jointly test for the significance of the lags on the explanatory variables, this in effect tests for 'Granger causality' between these variables. It is possible to have causality running from variable X to Y, but not Y to X; from Y to X, but not X to Y and from both Y to X and X to Y, although in this case interpretation of the relationship is difficult. The 'Granger causality' test can also be used as a test for whether a variable is exogenous i.e. if no variables in a model affect a particular variable it can be viewed as exogenous.

> ### *OLS Regression*

Ordinary least squares regression is the prevailing methodology used to test the hypotheses in this paper. The OLS regressions are defined as follows:

$$Y = \beta_1 + \beta_2 X_{2i} + ... + \beta_k X_{ki} + u_i \tag{15}$$

where X_2, X_3 and X_n are independent variables on which variable Y is dependent upon and u is the error term. The OLS regression is used to fit Y, X_2, X_3, …, X_k, in a sample of observations, the equation:

$$\hat{Y} = \beta_1 + \beta_2 X_{2i} + ... + \beta_k X_{ki} \tag{16}$$

Where the values of β_1, β_2, …, β_k are fitted into the model so that the sum of the residuals' squares is minimized. Thereby, the OLS regression provides a linear model to estimate the dependent variable Y.

4.3. Research results and Discussion

The aim with this section is to test the relationship between the accounting information and the CDS spreads in Bulgaria and to explain how well accounting data performs in predicting sovereign default.

> ### *Stationary*

Before proceeding to the regression models, we have applied panel unit root test:Summary. The results indicate that for all of the panel time series level data are not stationary so we have to transform them into first difference. The firs differences of the explored variables are trend- stationary so we may conclude that they are integrated in order one. The results from the test are presented in appendix VI. For the estimation of the first diiference of the explored variables, we use the following equation:

$$FirstDiff = \frac{VarValue_{it}}{VarValue_{it-1}} \tag{17}$$

Where:

FirstDiff- the first difference of the explored variable;

VarValue$_{it}$ - the value of the explored variables for the i- th country at moment t;

VarValue$_{it-1}$ - the value of the explored variable for the i- th country at the moment t-1.

OLS Regression model

Because of the fact that CDS prices may incorporate accounting information with a delay, we apply OLS regression by the following equation:

$$CDS_{it} = \alpha + \beta_1 Cash_{it-1} + \beta_2 Current_{it-1} + \beta_3 EBIT_{it-1} + \beta_4 Leverage_{it-1} +$$
$$\beta_5 LNSIZE_{it-1} + \beta_6 Riskfreerate_{it-1} + \beta_7 ROA_{it-1} + \beta_8 SalesAssets_{it-1} +$$
$$\beta_9 SalesCurrent_{it-1} + \beta_8 INTWO_{it-1} +$$
$$\varepsilon_{it} \quad (18)$$

INTWO is a dummy variable that measure consecutive losses. It gets value equal to 1 if net income is negative for two consecutive quarters and its value equal to 0 otherwise.

Table XXIV. Accounting variables as determinants of CDS spreads (Dependent variable CDS spreads)

Variable:	Expected sign:	Coefficient:	t- statistic:	p-value:
C		2.429089	3.655254	0.0003
Cash(-1)	Negative	-0.912606	-3.446432	0.0006
Current(-1)	Negative	-0.807334	-3.342060	0.0009
EBIT(-1)	Negative	0.001647	0.268314	0.7886
Leverage(-1)	Positive	-17.55491	-1.461979	0.1444
Lnsize(-1)	Negative	0.537354	0.226981	0.8205
Risk- free rate(-1)	Positive	17.43269	5.259675	0.0002
ROA (-1)	Negative	-12.51430	-0.808365	0.4193
SalesAssets(-1)	Negative	-6.833767	-3.750441	0.0002
SalesCurrent (-1)	Negative	-0.358336	-0.965268	0.3349
INTWO	Positive	0.767877	0.369102	0.7122
R- squared	0.073574			
Adjusted R- squared:	0.054782			
F-statistic	3.915239			
Probability	0.000038			

Source: Authors' calculations

The results in table XXIV provide that accounting data is able to provide statistical significant influence on CDS spreads. However, the R- squared value denotes that the accounting variables included in the model account for 7.35% of the variance of the CDS spreads. It represents a relative low level of explanatory power. Furthermore four out of the model's 10 explanatory variables are significant at the 1 % level and the variables' predicted signs are in line with the variables' actual signs of the coefficients.

Cash and *Current* are measurements of the operational liquidity and they are statistical significant. Their coefficients have negative signs, just as we have expected. The results suggest that the increased levels of liquidity will associate negatively with the CDS spreads. This suppose that the higher liquidity, the lower probability of sovereign default. It may due to the fact that if the liquidity deteriorates, the risk is exposed to increase. Consequently, the investors require higher CDS spreads in order to be compensated for the less liquidity market.

The *Sales- to- Assets* is the ratio, which is statistically significant, either. It has strong negative influence on CDS pricing, namely- its coefficient's value is (- 6.833767). Additionally Sivonen (2011) has pointed out that sales- to assets ratio may be accepted as a measurement of the effective usage of firm's assets in order to create sale revenue. He determines it as an indicator of managerial effectiveness, so it should have negative connection with default. These results suggest that liquidity of the explored firms is an important accounting variable in determining default probability when that is combined with other accounting variables. This conclusion is supported by the empirical findings in prior literature (see e.g. Sivonen 2011). According to Altman's model (1968), when combined with other accounting variables, sales- to- assets ratio is useful indicator in predicting default probability.

Risk- free- rate (Euribor 3m)- is the next statistically significant variable in the regression. Its sign is positive and its actual sign is in line with the predicted one. This is supported by CDS pricing theory, namely an increase in the risk- free rate results in higher CDS spreads. It means that sovereign CDS spreads of Bulgaria are sensitive to its macroeconomic conditions. Risk- free- rate (Euribor 3m) has a large positive effect on the Bulgarian CDS spreads. These explored positive relationship between CDS spreads and risk- free- rate is investigated by Mody (2009). A higher risk- free rate signals for more damaged global environment. Consequently it results into positive relationship between CDS and Euribor: the risk in the risk- free rate should be related to larger spreads on risky assets.

> *Vector autoregression model*

VAR estimation results with 8 lags are presented in **appendix VII**. Appendix VII shows impacts of lagged variables on the others. Furthermore, we estimate the relationship between accounting information and CDS spread with a VAR model where optimal number of lags is found to be eight according to Akaike information criterion.

Table XXV. VAR Lag Order Selection Criteria

Lag	LogL	LR	FPE	AIC	SC	HQ
0	-4825.941	NA	0.006737	26.21648	26.33306	26.26279
1	-4411.712	801.5162	0.001375	24.62716	26.02615*	25.18291
2	-4180.438	433.7170	0.000758	24.02947	26.71086	25.09465
3	-3755.809	771.0060	0.000147	22.38379	26.34758	23.95840
4	-3436.828	560.1625	5.06e-05	21.31072	26.55691	23.39476
5	-3043.420	667.4063	1.17e-05	19.83426	26.36285	22.42774
6	-2904.779	226.9354	1.08e-05	19.73864	27.54964	22.84155
7	-2468.890	687.5007	2.02e-06	18.03192	27.12532	21.64427
8	-2236.396	352.8368*	1.14e-06*	17.42762*	27.80342	21.54940*

Source: Authors' calculations.

> *VAR Model with CDS as dependent variable*

To examine the relation between accounting data and CDS spreads we apply VAR model. To start with we consider the VAR model with CDS as dependent variable. As we can see in the first eight rows of the first column (appendix 2) all the estimates (DCDS(1), DCDS(-2), DCDS(-3), DCDS(-4), DCDS(-5), DCDS(-6), DCDS(-7) and DCDS(-8)) are significant for the estimate for CDS spreads. Additionally, the overall explanatory power of the model is 95.63%. With other words, the dynamics of the CDS in the current moment could be explained with the dynamics of the CDS from the past periods. Considering the statistically significant T-statistics of DCASH (-1) with (2.70143) we are allowed to talk about the existence of impacts on DCDS. Consequently, the statistically significant cash to assets ratio is further evidence on the variable's ability to explain CDS spreads.

When considering the VAR model with CDS spread as dependent variable and *current ratio* as independent variable not much has changed. We find that current ratio from the previous period has an impact on the CDS spread in the current moment due to the statistically significant T-statistics of DCURRENT (-1) with (-3.70613). What is more, an extremely high current ratio can lead to the potential problems in the firms connecting with the firm's management that is not able to invest its surplus cash efficiently.

The VAR model includes two measures of profitability, EBIT and ROA. Based on our finding in appendix VII a negative relationship between DEBIT (-7) - the profitability variable and credit default swap spreads is discovered. R-squared of these variables shows that 0.956303 of changes in DCDS could be explained by these lagged values of indicators. On the other hand, return on assets ratio is one of the two independent variable that is not statistically significant - which further confirms that ROA do not have a significant influence on CDS spreads. Although increasing profitability is an encouraging sign of the company's business operations, the evidence implies that the return on a firm's assets is not of importance in default assessment.

Leverage (lev) in 8th lag is statistically significant, carries a T-statistics -2.02592 and a large coefficient value of (-9.391035).Thus, in addition to statistical significance, this result has some economic significance. Additionally, Ericsson, Jacobs and Oviedo (2009) suggest that leverage is perhaps the most relevant element in the probability of default.

On a similar note, firms' size, as measured by the natural logarithm of the value of total assets, influences CDS spreads.DLNSIZE(-4) has a large value of the coefficient (7.038916) and statistically significant T-statistics (2.16478) which leads to the conclusion that its impact on CDS spreads is noteworthy. These findings confirm that the credit markets consider larger firms as less likely to default. In fact, these results are in agreement with results obtained separated by Hillegeist and et. (2002) and Vassalou and Xing (2004).

Next, sales-to-assets variable (SalesAssets) is statistically significant in 1st, 5th, 6th, 7th and 8thlag considering VAR model. Consequently, the changes in credit default swap spreads could be explained bysales-to-assets variable due to the statistically significant T-statistics. The sales-to-assets ratio is a ratio that measures how well the firm is using its assets in order to make sales revenue. Thus it can be a sing of managerial efficiency and has logically a negative relationship with default. The obtained results confirm that liquidity is a significant variable in determining default probabilities.

In contrast, sales-to-current (SalesCurrent), which measures the current assets utilization rate, is the second independent variable that is not with statistically significant value at the VAR model. With other words, the dynamics of sales-to-current ratio does not have impact on the dynamics of the CDSs.

Consecutive losses were measured with the dummy variable INTWO. Interesting, we find the existence of a relationship between CDS spreads and INTWO (-2) estimating the VAR model with CDS as dependent variable. Therefore dummy variable INTWO has a predictive power on the dynamics of the CDS.

Finally, statistically significant T-statistics of DRISKFREE(-1)with 7.24335, DRISKFREE(-3) with (-42.4450), DRISKFREE(-4) with 27.2471,DRISKFREE(-5) with (-11.6845), DRISKFREE(-6) with (-2.26299), DRISKFREE(-7) with 5.80420 and DRISKFREE(-8) with 3.55679 allow us to talk about the existence of impacts on DCDS. We find that risk-free rate has a predictive capability for the dynamics of CDS. What is more, it seems reasonable to assume that CDS spreads are really sensitive to macroeconomic conditions. What is more, the macroeconomic sensitivity seems to reduce the somewhat marginal impact of the risk free rate in the pricing of CDSs. Increase in the risk- free- rate increase the expected future growth of the firm causing the market to rely on a higher level of firm value. Consequently, this leads to decrease in the probability of default. The results from the VAR tests, namely the negative signs and influence of risk- free- rate in CDS pricing, are supported by the ones of Fontana and Scheicher (2010). They reveal that the risk- free- rate possesses great significance on the highly unstable European economies. The lower interest rates are related to an unstable and weakening economy and it results in increasing credit spreads.

Table XXVI. Granger test in VAR

Dependent variable: DCDS				
Excluded	Chi-sq	df	Prob.	
DCASH	12.32134	8	0.1374	
DCURRENT	17.49588	8	0.0253	$Current \rightarrow CDS$
DEBIT	9.857707	8	0.2752	
DLEV	13.61149	8	0.0925	
DLNSIZE	13.70387	8	0.0898	
DRISKFREE	2897.273	8	0.0000	$Riskfreerate \rightarrow CDS$
DROA	7.471896	8	0.4867	
DSALESASSETS	164.7260	8	0.0000	$SalesAssets \rightarrow CDS$
DSALESCURRENT	32.46549	8	0.0001	$SalesCurrent \rightarrow CDS$
All	4764.546	72	0.0000	

Source: Authors' calculations.

The results from Granger test in autoregressive conditions are presented in table XXVI and they confirm the results not only from VAR test, but the ones from OLS regression. We prove that CDS dynamics is influenced by current ratio, risk- free rate, sales assets and sales current at 5 % level of significance. All of the aforementioned accounting variables granger cause CDS in VAR.

> *VAR Model with CASH/ CURRENT/ EBIT/ LEV/ LNSIZE/ RISKFREE/ ROA/ SALESASSETS/ SALESCURRENT/ INTWO as dependent variable*

The picture is different when considering the VAR model with CASH ratio as dependent variable. We see that DCDS does not influence the dynamics of DCash due to the statistically insignificant values of T-statistics. We reach to identical results when the dependent variable is successively DEBIT, DLEV and DLNSIZE taking into account the statistically insignificant values of T-statistics. Here, we can assume that the changes in these variables could not be explained by CDS spread. In the third column, statistically significant T-statistics of DCDS(-8) with 2.29403 allow us to claim about the existence of impacts on DCURRENT. Therefore, the CDS dynamics can impact the current ratio which measures the liquidity. Further, we note that there is an influence not only from DRISKFREE to DCDS, but also vice versa. What is more, CDS is statistically significant in 2nd, 3rd, 4th, 6th, 7th and 8th lag considering VAR model. We find that the CDS spread dynamics have an impact on the profitability, measured by ROA ratio. Also, statistically significant T-statistics of DCDS(-2) with 2.49462, DCDS(-3) with -2.10856 and DCDS(-5) with 5.80677 is a proof of the existence of impacts on DSALESASSETS, measuring the asset utilization. Finally, the CDS can influence the current asset utilization and consecutive losses.

Conclusion

Summing up the results of the analysis, it can be concluded that SEE capital markets are highly related, which also shows co-movement in their market dynamics. The degree of development of the capital markets also determines the linkages between them, showing that the reference ones demonstrate a lower positive correlation than the developing ones. The Serbian market is most highly correlated in the group, and the least correlated - Banja Luka. One of the possible reasons for the weak connection between Banja Luka and the other examined countries is the fact that the Banja Luka market is small and illiquid and the access of foreign investors to it is very limited. The Bulgarian capital market is synchronized with the other SEE markets because of the high or average positive values of registered correlation coefficients and the stronger influence of the Greek innovations. These results are proved by the VAR analysis. It is revealed high degree of interaction of the Bulgarian, Romanian and Serbian capital markets with the reference capital markets of this group of countries. We prove high degree of integration of the Bulgarian, Romanian and Serbian capital markets among the reference capital markets of this group of countries. It is proved fast degree of information incorporation for reference and developing capital markets from the other members of the group. We should mention that we observe less significant interactions between reference capital markets than the ones between developing. These results confirm the ones from the correlation analysis. The developing capital markets of the explored group are strongly determined by country- specific factors, but five of them are strongly influenced by the Greek innovations. However, the market integration is anticipated to strengthen, as a result of EU expansion, as the implementation of Strategy 2020. These results lead to the argument that investor can benefit, at least in the short run, from diversifying into the SEE equity markets. All things consider, we can assume that the Southeast European capital markets are characterized with synchronicity and co-movement of stock market dynamics, which is the first step towards achieving market integration. We should be careful with the fact that the deeper financial integration corresponds to a greater cost of financial contagion, implying a concession between them. Following these conclusions: due to the revealed interdependences between the explored capital markets, foreign investors may benefit by including stocks of these countries in their investing portfolios. These countries will take profit if their capital markets are more accessible to foreign investors, reorganizing them in conditions to international law in order to defend foreign investors.

Summarizing the empirical results of the analysis the linkages between the capital market and the public expectations, including inflation expectations, consumer and business confidence, several conclusions can be made:

❖ There is empirically more evidence of a linkage between business confidence and capital markets, regardless of its direction, than between consumer confidence and capital markets. In just four countries, there is a relation between capital markets and consumer confidence, but when it is replaced by business confidence, statistically significant links are found for all of the examined countries.

❖ Four of the SEE countries - Bulgaria, Macedonia, Romania, Slovenia registered a statistically significant relation "capital market - business confidence" except as less efficient according to the EMH, but also as predisposed to a more dynamic reflection of the impact of market impulses during the crisis periods.

❖ In markets with the highest values of market capitalization is available line of influence "business confidence - capital market". This determines the capital markets of Turkey, Greece and Croatia as effective and more comprehensive in the context of the Efficient Market Hypothesis. Thus confirming the hypothesis assumptions about the relationship between the degree of market development and the transfer of information to the market prices and returns as the last and critical exponents of all available information. This assumption of market efficiency in more developed capital markets also reflects the assumptions of Real Business Cycle Theory, which implies transferring influences from the real to the financial sector only, but not vice versa.

❖ Anylizing the relationship between consumer confidence and capital markets we can make a conclusion that its direction is determined by the degree of development of the capital market. In the reference Croatian and Greek markets, the influence is from consumer confidence towards capital market, while in the developing Bulgarian and Slovenian markets it is opposite – from capital market towards consumer confidence. If the registered for more developed markets is in line with the Keynesian model of economic growth assumptions, the question of why this determinant role of consumer confidence does not work according to model requirements is raised in emerging markets. One explanation may come from the disposable income. If income is low and relatively constant, it reduces the weight and importance of disposable income for aggregate consumption and GDP dynamics. Another explanation could be given in terms of the paradox of saving. If consumers consider the capital market as a source of information for the development of the economy, all negative impulses there will lead to a subsequent impact on consumer confidence leading to increased savings, which ultimately prevents consumer confidence from being a leading determinant of aggregate spending , but turns it into a follower variable depending on the dynamics of GDP. The Milton Friedman permanent income hypothesis could generate an explanation if we assume that the income level is relatively constant and above the long-term expectation, i. e. consumers have negative future expectations about their income and therefore saving is increasing. Enhancing this effect, i.e. of the negative expectations of future permanent income, could explain the existence of the statistically significant link "capital market - consumer confidence" for Bulgaria and Slovenia.

❖ The registered influences on the capital market line - consumer (for Bulgaria and Slovenia) and business (for Bulgaria, Macedonia, Romania and Slovenia) trust violate the assumptions of the Real Business Cycle Theory. This could identify these emerging markets as less efficient in terms of this theory, as far as they allow information influence from an external factor - the capital market, a representative of the financial sector.

❖ The capital market dynamics of Greek market influence the inflation expectations.

❖ We prove that the happiness of the consumers is important not only for capital markets but for sovereign credit risk. The consumer confidence is an indicator which may predict and provoke a turmoil of economic activity. As it was proved, falling confidence is not favorable towards equities as it is an indication of declining business sales. Consequently, in the case of Bulgaria, consumer confidence should be considered as an economic indicator which derives most of its information content from past and current economic outlook. This is especially true during the financial crisis of 2008 when the future is uncertain and risky.This confirms the hypothesis that sentiment indicators possesses a role of common or systematic risk factors of CDS spread changes. The significant results may be considered as a confirmation of the multiple-equilibria theory, namely that financial markets may take optimal behaviours sometimes during a period of turmoil and this leads to self-fulfilling liquidity crisis and self-fulfilling prophecies. that sentiment variables may explain CDS spread changes efficiently. We observe bilateral relations, which may be accepted as proves that turmoil periods may be led by panic and fear of investors without any enormous change in other factors. The increasing default probability of Bulgaria tends to lead to increase in investors' fear and panic. We accept this as a prove of the realization of the "snowball effect". The bilateral relationship between SOFIX and CDS reveals a transmission channel between "private sector" and "public sector".

Proving the strong influence of sentiment indicators in Bulgaria, we reveal the fundamental determinants of CDS spreads in Bulgaria and Romania. One of the main contributions of this research is that in addition to variables that proxy for global and macroeconomic CDS spreads determinants, we also employ variables that proxy for behavioral determinants.

Fluctuations of global financial and behavioral variables dominate in explaining CDS pricing change so, it means that systematic risk has stronger influence in CDS pricing than the individual risk. In conditions of systematic risk influence, the Euro zone membership leads to increase in CDS spreads. This means that being members of the Euro zone, countries will be strongly affected by the systematic risk and contagion effects. When we explore, macroeconomic determinants influence, the Euro zone membership neutralizes the effects of the debt level and local capital markets and reduces CDS spreads. When exploring global variables effects- in these cases when the country is not a Euro zone member, global determinants are neutralized by the value of the Euro zone membership's coefficient. The country- specific variables, such as inflation, debt/GDP, current account/ GDP, local capital markets' indexes – have an explanatory power, either but it is less strong than the explanatory power of the global determinants. These results are consistent with the results of Pan and Singleton (2008), Fontana and Scheicher (2010), Longstaff et al. (2011) and Alper et al. (2012), which mean that CDS spreads are strongly connected to global risk determinants, rather than macroeconomic and country-specific variables. We also report evidence that sentiment may play role in CDS spread determination, along with other facts, but they are not significant in determining the Euro zone membership probability. These results confirm the ones of Fontana and Scheicher's (2010). This analysis suggests that the traditional measures (Merton's model) of sovereign default risk are not sufficient to measure it. The Euro zone variable possesses a significant power in CDS spreads determining and vice- versa.

Another main contribution of this paper is the fact that it explores the relevance of accounting information to debt markets which has not been studied to a large extent.

Secondly, the prior researches on the relationship between credit risk literature and accounting data has concentrated on the U.S markets whereas our research is focused on Bulgarian markets.

To our knowledge this is the first paper which examines the relationship between accounting data and sovereign credit default swap spreads. We reveal that accounting data is a relevant source of information to the credit and debt markets. More precisely, it is proved that our accounting- based model designed to measure the relevance of accounting information in general is able to explain about 7 % of the variation in sovereign CDS spreads. So we may conclude that accounting information is proved to provide incremental influence to the probability of default in Bulgaria.

As a result, this study has shown that CDS spreads has a significant relationship with other accounting and market variables and VAR model is a useful model to make strategic forecasts by using lagged variables. All things considered, liquidity, profitability, leverage, size, risk-free rate, asset utilization and consecutive losses for the twenty Bulgarian firms have an impact on the dynamics of the credit default spread. This study finds convincing evidence that accounting information is a relevant source of information to the credit markets.

REFERENCES

[1] Abid, F. and N. Naifar. 2006. *"The determinants of credit default swap rates: An explanatory study"*. International Journal of Theoretical and Applied Finance, 09(01), pp. 23-42.

[2] Aga, M. and B. Kocaman. 2011. *"Efficient Market Hypothesis and Emerging Capital Markets: Empirical Evidence from Istanbul Stock Exchange"*, Journal of Financial Markets Research, pp. 44-57.

[3] Aggarwal, R. and Kyaw, N. A. 2004. *"Equity Market Integration in the NAFTA Region: Evidence from Unit Root and Cointegration Tests"*. SSRN Electronic Journal.

[4] Aizenman, J., Hutchison, M., Jinjarak, Y., 2013. *"What is the risk of European sovereigndebt defaults? Fiscal space, CDS spreads and market pricing of risk"*. J. Int. MoneyFinanc. 34 (C), pp. 37–59.

[5] Alper, C. Emre, Lorenzo Forni and Marc Gerard. 2012. *"Pricing of Sovereign Credit Risk: Evidence from Advanced Economies During the Financial Crisis"*. IMF Working Paper, No. 12/24.

[6] Altman, E. 1968. "Financial Ratios, Discriminant Analysis and the Prediction of Corporat eBankruptcy", Journal of Finance, 23, pp. 589-609.

[7] Armeanu, D. and S. Cioaca. 2014. *"Testing the Efficient Markets Hypothesis on the Romanian Capital Market"*, Proceedings of the 8th Management challenges for sustainable development international conference, November 6th-7th, 2014, Bucharest, Romania, pp. 252-261.

[8] Aunon- Nerin, D., D. Cossin, T. Hricko and Z. Huang. 2002.*"Exploring the Determinants of Credit Risk in Credit Default Swap Transaction Data: Is Fixed Income Market Information Sufficient to Evaluate Credit Risk?"* (Working paper (FAME))

[9] Babetskii, I., Komarek L. and Komarkova, Z. 2007. *"Financial Integration of Stock Markets among New EU Member States and the Euro Area"*.Czech Journal of Economics and Finance, 57(7-8), pp. 341-362. Available at: https://doi.org/10.1108/SEF-04-2012-0048

[10] Baek, I.-M., Bandopadhyaya, A., Du, C., 2005. Determinants of marketassessedsovereign risk: economic fundamentals or market risk appetite? J. Int. MoneyFinanc. 24 (4), pp. 533–548.

[11] Baldacci, E., Gupta, S., Mati, A. 2011. *"Political and fiscal risk determinants ofsovereign spreads in emerging markets?"* , Rev. Dev. Econ. Vol.15 No:2, pp. 251–263.

[12] Baldacci, E., S. Gupta and Mati A. 2008. *"Is it (Still) Mostly Fiscal? Determinants of Sovereign Spreads in Emerging Markets"*, IMF Working Paper, No. 08/259.

[13] Ball, R., and P. Brown. 1968. "An Empirical Evaluation of Accounting Income Numbers", Journal of Accounting Research, pp. 159-178.

[14] Barber, B. M., and T. Odean. 2008. *"All that glitters: The efect of attention and news on the buying behavior of individual and institutional investors"*, Review of Financial Studies, 21(2), pp. 785-818.

[15] Batta, G., Ganguly and J. Rosett. 2002. *"Financial Statement Recasting and Credit Risk Assessment"* (Working Paper).

[16] Baumohl, B. 2012. *"The secrets of economic indicators: hidden clues to future economic trends and investment opportunities"*, Upper Saddle River, New Jersey: FT Press.

[17] Baur, D. and Jung, R. C. 2006. *"Return and volatility linkages between the US and the German stock market"*, Journal of International Money and Finance, 25(4), pp. 598-613.

[18] Beaver, W., Clarke, R., and W. Wright. 1979.*"The Association Between Unsystematic Security Returnsand the Magnitude of Earnings Forecast Errors"*, Journal of Accounting Research, pp. 316-340.

[19] Beirne, J., Fratzscher, M. 2013. *"The pricing of sovereign risk and contagion during the European sovereign debt crisis"*. J. Int. Money Financ. 34 (C), pp. 60–82.

[20] Benkert, C. 2004. *"Explaining credit default swap premia"*, J. Fut. Mark., 24, pp. 71–92. doi:10.1002/fut.10112.

[21] Black, F. and J. C. Cox. 1976. *"Valuating corporate securities: some effects of bond identure provisions"*, The Journal of Finance,31, pp. 351–367.

[22] Blommestein, H., Eijffinger, S., Qian, Z. 2015. *"Regime dependent determinants of Euro area sovereign CDS spreads"*, Journal of Financial Stability, No.22, pp. 10-21

[23] Boehmer, E., Megginson, W.L. 1990. *"Determinants of Secondary Market Prices for Developing Country Syndicated Loans?"*, J. Financ. Vol.45 No.5, pp. 1517–1540

[24] Borges, M. R. 2010. *"Efficient market hypothesis in European stock market"*, The European Journal of Finance, 1607, pp.711-726.

[25] Breitenfellner,B., and Wagner, N. 2012. *"Explaining Aggregate Credit Default Swap Spread"*, International Review of Financial analysis. Vol.22, pp. 18-29

[26] Callen, J., J. Livnat, and D. Segal. 2009. *"The Impact of Earnings on the Pricing of Credit Default Swaps"*, Accounting Review, *84*, pp. 1363-1394.

[27] Cappieollo, L., Gerard B., Kadareja, A. and Manganelli, S. 2006. *"Financial Integration of New EU Member States"*.European Central Bank Working Paper No. 683.

[28] Černý, A. and Koblas, M. 2008. *"Stock Market Integration and the Speed of Information Transmission"*. Czech Journal of Economics and Finance, 58(1-2), pp. 2-20. Available at: http://journal.fsv.cuni.cz/storage/1098_str_2_20_-_cerny-koblas.pdf

[29] Chakravarty, S. *"Conservatism Flow and the Pricing of Credit Deault Swaps"*. 2010 (Working Paper (California State University, Fullerton))

[30]   Chong, T.L., Wong, Y.C. and Yan, K.-M. 2008. *"International linkages of the Japanese stock market"*, Japan and the World Economy, 20, pp. 601–621.

[31]   Cifarelli, G. and Paladino, G. 2005. *"Volatility linkages across three major equity markets: A financial arbitrage approach"*, Journal of International Money and Finance, 24(3), pp. 413-439.

[32]   Cohen, L., and A. Frazzini. 2008. *„Economic links and predictable returns"*, Journal of Finance, 63(4), pp. 1977-2011.

[33]   Collin-Dufresne, P, R Goldstein and JS Martin. 2001. *„The Determinants of Credit SpreadChanges"*, Journal of Finance, 56, pp. 2177–2207.

[34]   Corredor, P., Ferrer, E and Santamaria, Rafael. (2015). *"The Impact of Investor Sentiment on Stock Returns in Emerging Markets: The Case of Central European Markets"*, Eastern European Economics, 53, pp. 328-355.

[35]   Coudert, Virgine, and Mathieu Gex. 2006. *"Can risk aversion indicators anticipate financial crises?"*, Banque de France, Financial Stability Review, 9.

[36]   Curtin, R. 2007. *"Consumer Sentiment Surveys: Worldwide Review and Assessment"*, Journal of Business Cycle Measurement and Analysis 3(1), pp. 7-42.

[37]   Dailami, M., Masson, P.R., Padou, J.J. 2008. *"Global monetary conditions versuscountry-specific factors in the determination of emerging market debt spreads?"*, J. Int. Money Finance. Vol.27, No 8, pp. 1325–1336.

[38]   Darrat, A. and Zhong, M. 2005. *"Equity Market Linkage and Multinational Trade Accords: The Case of NAFTA"*, Journal of International Finance and Money, 24(5), pp. 793-817.

[39]   Das, R, P Hanouna, and A. Sarin. 2009. *"Accounting-Based versus Market-Based Cross-Sectional Models of CDS Spreads"*, Journal of Banking & Finance, 33, pp. 719-730.

[40]   Das, S. R . 1995. *"Credit Risk Derivatives"*, Journal of Derivatives,. 2(3), pp. 7-23.

[41]   Das, S., and R. K. Sundaram. 2000. *"Of Smiles and Smirks: A Term Structure Perspective"*, Journal of Financial and Quantitative Analysis, 34 (02), pp. 211-239.

[42]   Della Vigna, S., and J. M. Pollet. 2009. *"Investor inattention and Friday earnings announcements"*, Journal of Finance, 64(2), pp. 709-749.

[43]   Demirovic, A., and D. Thomas. 2007. *"The Relevance of Accounting Data in the Measurement of Credit Risk"*, The European Journal of Finance, 33, pp. 253-268.

[44]   Dieckmann, S., Plank, T. 2011. *"Default risk of advanced economies: an empiricalanalysis of credit default swaps during the financial crisis"*, Rev. Financ., pp. 1–32

[45]   Ding, Z., C.W.J. Granger and R.F. Engle, 1993. *"A Long Memory Property of Stock Market Returns and a New Model"*, Journal of Empirical Finance, 1, pp. 83-106.

[46]   Dragota, V. and D.S. Oprea. 2014. *"Informational efficiency tests on the Romanian stock market: a review of the literature"*, The Review of Finance and Banking, 06 (1), pp. 015-028.

[47]   Duffie, D. and K. J. Singleton. 1999. *"Modeling the term structure of defaultable bonds"*, Review of Financial Studies, 12, pp. 687-720.

[48]   Duffie, D., and D. Lando. 2001. "Term Structure of Credit Spreads With Incomplete Accounting Information." Econometrica, 69, pp. 633-664.

[49]   Easley, D., M. O'hara, and P. S. Srinivas. 1998. *"Option volume and stock prices: Evidence on where informed traders trade"*, Journal of Finance, 53(2), pp. 431-465.

[50]   Edwards, S. 1984. "The Order of Liberalization of the Current and Capital Accounts of the Balance of Payments", NBER Working Papers 1507, National Bureau of Economic Research, Inc.

[51]   Egert, B. and Kocenda, E. 2007. *"Interdependencs between Eastern and Western European stock markets: Evidence from intraday data"*, Economic Systems, 31(2), pp. 184-203. Available at: doi:10.1016/j.ecosys.2006.12.004.

[52]   Ericsson, J., K. Jacobs, and R. Oviedo. 2009. "The Determinants of Credit Default Swap Premia", Journal of Financial & Quantitative Analysis, *44*, pp. 109-132.

[53]   E-Views Help System. 2018. Quantitative Micro Software, http://www.eviews.com.

[54]   Flannery, M., J. 2010. *"Credit Default Swap Spreads as Variable Substitutes for Credit Ratings"*, Conference Paper, University of Pennsylvania Law Reviewand the Institute for Law and Economic Policy, 2010.

[55]   Fontana, A. and M. Scheicher. 2010. *"An Analysis of Euro Area Sovereign CDS and Their Relation with Government Bonds"*, European Central Bank Working Paper Series, No.12, 2010.

[56]   Forbes, K. and Rigobon, R. 2002. *"No contagion, Only Interdependence: Measuring Stock Market Comovements"*, Journal of Finance, 57(5), pp. 2223-2261. Available at: http://dx.doi.org/10.1111/0022-1082.00494.

[57]   Forte, S., and J. Pena. 2009. *"Credit spreads: An empirical analysis on the informational content of stocks, bon and CDS"*, Journal of Banking and Finance, pp. 2013-2022.

[58]   Forte, S., and L. Lovreta. 2009. *"Credit Risk Discovery in the Stock and CDS Markets: Who Leads, When, and Why"* Available at SSRN: https://ssrn.com/abstract=1183202 or http://dx.doi.org/10.2139/ssrn.1183202 , 2009.

[59]   Fujii, E. 2005. *"Intra and inter-regional causal linkages of emerging stock markets: evidence from Asia and Latin America in and out of crises"*, Journal of International Financial Markets, Institutions and Money, 15 (3), pp. 315–342.

[60]   Ganchev, G. 2015. *"Towards Holistic Theory of Money: Overcoming twentieth century neoclassical monetary paradigm"*, Economic Study, 4, pp. 3- 24.

[61]　　Gapen, M., D.F. Gray, C. H. Lim and Xiao,Y. 2005. *"Measuring and Analyzing Sovereign Risk with Contingent Claims"*, IMF Working Paper, No. 05/155.

[62]　　Geamănu, M. 2014. *"VAR analysis on Foreign Direct Investment in Romania"*, Theoretical and Applied Economics, Volume XXI (2014), 4(593), pp. 39-52.

[63]　　Georgantopoulos, A. G., D. F. Kenourgios and A. D. Tsamis, 2011. *"Calendar anomalies in emerging Balkan equity markets"*, International economics & finance journal, 6 (1), pp. 67-82.

[64]　　Gerunov, A., 2014. *"Linkages between Public Sentiments and Stock Market Dynamics in the Context of the Efficient Market Hypothesis"*, Economic and Social Alternatives, 3, pp. 58-71. (in Bulgarian)

[65]　　Geshkov, M. 2014. *"The Effect of the World Economic Crisis on the Countries of the Balkan Region"*, Economic Alternatives, 1, pp. 108-125. http://www.unwe.bg/uploads/Alternatives/10_Geshkov_1_2014.pdf.

[66]　　Gilmore, C. G. and McManus, G. M. 2004. *"The impact of NAFTA on the integration of the Canadian, Mexican and U.S. equity markets"*, Research in Global Strategic Management, 10, pp. 137–151.

[67]　　Gilmore, C., Lucey, B. and McManus, G. 2008. *"The Dynamics of Central European Equity Market Integration"*, Quarterly Review of Economics and Finance, 48(3), pp. 605-622. Available at: https://doi.org/10.1016/j.qref.2006.06.005.

[68]　　Glosten, L.R., R. Jagannathan and D. Runkle. 1993. *"On the Relation Between the Expected Value and the Volatility of the Nominal Excess Return on Stocks"*, Journal of Finance, 48, pp. 1779-1801.

[69]　　Görmüş, Ş. And S. Güneş. 2010. *"Consumer Confidence, Stock Prices and Exchange Rates: The Case of Turkey"*, Econometrics and International Development, Vol. 10, pp. 113-124 ISSN:1578-4487.

[70]　　Gradojevic, N. and Dobardzic, E. 2013. *"Causality between Regional Stock Markets: A Frequency Domain Approach"*, Panoeconomicus, 5, pp. 633-647. Available at: doi: 10.2298/PAN1305633G.

[71]　　Greatrex, C. A. 2009. *"Credit Default Swap Market Determinants"*, The Journal of Fixed Income, 18 (3), pp. 18-32; DOI: https://doi.org/10.3905/JFI.2009.18.3.018

[72]　　Hillegeist, S, E Keating, D. Cram, and K. Lundstedt. 2002.*"Assessing the Probability of Bankruptcy"*, Working paper, The Kellog School, Northwestern University.

[73]　　Hilscher, J., Pollet, J. and M. Wilson. 2015. *"Are Credit Default Swaps a Sideshow? Evidence That Information Flows from Equity to CDS Markets"*. Journal of Financial and Quantitative Analysis, 50(3), pp. 543-567. doi:10.1017/S0022109015000228

[74]　　Horvath, R. and Petrovski, D. 2013. *"International Stock market integration: Central and South Eastern Europe compared"*. IOS Working Paper, No.317.

[75]   Huang, J., and M. Huang. 2003. *"How Much of the Corporate-Treasury Yield Spread is Dueto Credit Risk?"*, Review of Asset Pricing Studies, 2, pp. 153-202.

[76]   Hull, J., and A. White. 2000. *"The Impact of Default Risk on the Prices of Options and Other Derivative Securities"*, Journal of Banking and Finance, *19*, pp. 299-322.

[77]   IMF, 2013. *Global Financial Stability Report: Old Risks, New Challenges, Technical report,* International Monetary Fund.

[78]   Ivanov, I., B. Lomev, B. Bogdanova. 2012. *"Investigation of the market efficiency of emerging stock markets in the East-European region"*, International Journal of Applied Operational Research, 2(2), pp. 13-24, doi:http://www.ijorlu.ir/browse.php?mag_id=5&slc_lang=en&sid=1.

[79]   Jarrow, R. and S. Turnbull. 1995. *"Pricing derivatives on financial securities subject to default risk"*, Journal of Finance, *50, pp. 53-86.*

[80]   Jarrow, R.A., D. Landoand S. M. Turnbull. 1997.*"Amarkov model for the term structure of credit risk spreads"*, The review of financial Studies, 10, pp. 481-523.

[81]   Johnson, R. and Soenen, L. 2003. *"Economic integration and stock market comovements in the Americas"*. Journal of Multinational Financial Management, 13(1), pp. 85-100. Available at: https://doi.org/10.1016/S1042-444X(02)00035-X.

[82]   Kasch-Haroutounian, M. and Price, S. 2001. *"Volatility in the Transition Markets of Central Europe"*, Applied Financial Economics, 11(1), pp. 93-105. Available at: http://dx.doi.org/10.1080/09603100150210309.

[83]   Kenourgios, D. and Samitas, A. 2011. *"Equity market integration in emerging Balkan markets"*, Research in International Business and Finance, 25(3), pp. 296-307. Available at: doi:10.1016/j.ribaf.2011.02.004.

[84]   Kocenda, E. and Egert, B. 2011. *"Time-Varying Synchronization of European Stock Markets"*, Empirical Economics, 40(2), pp. 393-407. Available at: doi: 10.1007/s00181-010-0341-3.

[85]   Kolstad, M. 2013. *"An analysis of Euro zone sovereign credit default swaps"*, Master's thesis. Copenhagen Business School.

[86]   Lamont, O. and A. Frazzini, 2007. *"The Earnings Announcement Premium and Trading Volume,"* NBER Working Papers 13090, National Bureau of Economic Research, Inc.

[87]   Levin, A., Chien-Fu, L. and J. Ch. Chia-Shang. 2002. *"Unit root tests in panel data: asymptotic and finite-sample properties"*, Journal of Econometrics, Elsevier, 108(1), pp. 1-24.

[88]   Li, H. and Majerowska, E. 2008. *"Testing stock market linkages for Poland and Hungary: A multivariate GARCH approach"*, Research in International Business and Finance, 22 (3), pp. 247–266.

[89]   Lim, L. K. 2009. *"Convergence and interdependence between ASEAN-5 stock markets"*, Mathematics and Computers in Simulation, 79(9), pp. 2957–2966.

[90] Longin, F. and Solnik, B. 1995. *"Is the correlation in international equity returns constant: 1960-1990?"*, Journal of International Money and Finance, 14(1), pp. 3-26. Available at: https://doi.org/10.1016/0261-5606(94)00001-H.

[91] Longin, F. and Solnik, B. 2001. *"Extreme correlation of international equity markets"*, Journal of Finance, 56, pp. 649-676.

[92] Longstaff, F. A. and E. S. Schwartz. 1995. *"A Simple Approach to Valuing Risky Fixed and Floating Rate Debt."* The Journal of Finance, 50, pp. 789–819.

[93] Longstaff, F. A., J. Pan, Pedersen, L.H. and Singleton, K.J., 2011. *"How Sovereign is Sovereign Credit Risk?"*, American Economic Journal: Macroeconomics, Vol. 3, No.2, pp. 75-103.

[94] Merton, R. C. 1974. *"On the pricing of corporate debt: The risk structure of interest rates"*, The Journal of Finance, 2, pp. 449- 470.

[95] Miljković, V. and O. Radović. 2006. *"Stylized facts of asset returns: case of BELEX"*, Facta Universitatis, Series: Economics and Organization, 3 (2), pp. 189–201.

[96] Mody, A. 2009. *"From Bear Sterns to AngloIrish: How Eurozone Sovereign Spreads Related to Financial Sector Vulnerabiity"*, IMF Working Paper 09/108.

[97] Nelson, D. 1991. *"Conditional heteroskedasticity in asset returns: a new approach"*, Econometrics, 59, pp. 349–370.

[98] Norden, L., and M. Weber. 2004. *"The Comovement of Credit Default Swap, Bond and Stock Markets: An Empirircal Analysis"*, Center of Financial Studies, № 2004/20.

[99] OECD, 2012. *OECD Sovereign Borrowing Outlook,* OECD Publishing.

[100] Ohlosn, J. 1980. *"Financial Ratios and the Probabilistic Prediction of Bankruptcy",* Journal of Accounting Research, 18, pp. 109-131.

[101] O'Kane, D., and S. Turnbull. 2003. *"Valuation of Credit Default Swaps",* Fixed income quantitativeresearch, Lehman Brothers.

[102] Oprea, D.Ş. and L. Brad. 2013. *"Investor sentiment and stock returns: Evidence from Romania"*, International Journal of Academic Research in Accounting, Finance and Management Sciences, 4(2), pp. 23-29.

[103] Pan, J. and K. J. Singleton, K.J. 2008. *"Default and Recovery Implicit in the Term Structure of Sovereign CDS Spreads"*, The Journal of Finance, Vol. 63, pp. 2345-2384.

[104] Patonov, N. 2016. *"Fiscal Impacts on Output in a Small Open Economy: The Case of Albania"*, Scientific Annals of Economics and Business 63 (2), pp. 161- 169. DOI: 10.1515/saeb-2016-0113.

[105] Samitas, A., D. Kenourgios and N. Paltalidis. 2011. *"Equity market integration in Balkan emerging markets"*, Research in International Business and Finance, 25(3), pp. 296–307.

[106] Schwert, G.W. 1989. *"Why Does Stock Market Volatility Change Over Time?"*, Journal of Finance, 44, pp. 1115-1153.

[107] Sellin, P. 2001. *"Monetary policy and the stock market: theory and empirical evidence"*, Journal of Economic Surveys, 15(4), pp. 491–541.

[108] Shachmurove, Y. 2005. *"Dynamic Linkages Among the Emerging Middle Eastern and the United States Stock Markets"*, International Journal of Business.

[109] Shumway, T. 2001. *"Forecasting Bankruptcy More Accurately: A Simple Hazard Model"*, The Journal of Business, 74, pp. 101-24.

[110] Simeonov, S. 2015. *"Stock Exchange and Economic Activity Indicators – Relations and Asymmetry during the Recession in Serbia and Bulgaria"*, Financial Markets and the Real Economy: Some Reflections on the Recent Financial Crisis, ISBN: 978-86-6139-097-5, pp. 59-77.

[111] Sivonen, A. 2011. *"The Relevance of Accounting versus Market Information in Credit Risk Measurment- European Credit Default Swap Evidence"*. Aalto University master thesis.

[112] Spyrou, S. Galariotis, E.G., Makrichoti, P. 2016. *"Sovereign CDS spread determinants and spill-over effects during financial crisis: A panel VAR approach"*, Journal of Financial Stability (26), pp. 62-77

[113] Spyrou, S. 2013. *"Investor sentiment and yield spread determinants: evidence from European markets"*, Journal of Economic Studies, 40(6), pp. 739 – 762.

[114] Stavrova, E. 2017. *"Conventional and Shadow Banking Sector- Comparative aspects of the Post- crisis Period in Taim of the Currency Board- Bulgaria's Case"*, CBU International Conference of Innovations in Science and Education, Vol. 5, Prague, Czech Republic, pp. 453- 457.

[115] Stoica, O. and Diaconasu, D. 2013. *"Analysis of interdependencies between Austrian and CEE stock markets"*. Faculty of Economics and Business Administration, Romania.

[116] Stoica, O., Perry, M. J. and Mehdian, S. 2015. *"An empirical analysis of the diffusion of information across stock markets of Central and Eastern Europe"*. Prague Economic Papers, 24(2), pp. 192-210. DOI: http://dx.doi.org/10.18267/j.pep.508.

[117] Stoilova, D. 2017. *"Tax Structure and Economic Growth: Evidence from the European Union"*, Contraduria y Admini stracion, 62, pp. 1041- 1057.

[118] Syllignakis, M. N. and Kouretas, G. P. 2010. *"German, US and Central and Eastern European Stock Market Integration"*, Open Economies Review, 21(4), pp. 607-628.

[119] Syriopoulos, T. 2007. *"Dynamic linkages between emerging European and developed stock markets: Has the EMU any impact?"*, International Review of Financial Analysis, 16 (1), pp. 41– 60.

[120] Syriopoulos, T. and Roumpis, E. 2009. *"Dynamic correlations and volatility effects in the Balkan equity markets"*. Journal of International Financial Markets, Institutions and Money, 19(4), pp. 565–587.

[121]   Tanchev, S. 2016. *"The Role of the Proportional Income Tax on Economic Growth of Bulgaria"*, Economic Studies, 4, pp. 66-77.

[122]   Tang, D.Y., and Yan, H. 2010. *"Market conditions, default risk and credit spreads"*, Journal of Banking and Finance, 743- 753

[123]   Taylor, S.J. 1986. *"Modeling Financial Time Series. Chichester"*, UK: John Wiley and Sons.

[124]   Todorov, I. 2017. *"Bulgaria's Cyclical Position and Market (DIS) Equilibria"*, Economic Studies, 5, pp. 30-64.

[125]   Tsenkov, V. 2015. *"Crisis influences between developed and developing capital markets - the case of central and eastern European countries"*. Economic Studies, 3, pp. 71-108.

[126]   Tsenkov, V. and Stoitsova-Stoykova, A. 2017. *"The impact of the global financial crisis on the market efficiency of capital markets of South East Europe"*. International Journal of Contemporary Economics and Administrative Sciences, 7(1-2), pp. 31-57. http://www.ijceas.com/index.php/ijceas/article/view/146/pdf

[127]   Vassalou, M, and Y. Xing. 2004. *"Default Risk in Equity Returns"*, The Journal of Finance, *59*, pp. 831-868.

[128]   Voronkova, S. 2004. *"Equity market integration in Central European emerging markets: A cointegration analysis with shifting regimes"*, International Review of Financial Analysis, 13(5), pp. 633-647. Available at:http://dx.doi.org/10.12775/DEM.2012.002.

[129]   Wang, J., Fu, G., and C. Luo. 2013. *"Accounting information and stock price reaction of listed companies—empirical evidence from 60 listed companies in Shanghai Stock Exchange"*. Journal of Business & Management, 2(2).

[130]   Yang, T. and Lim, J. 2004. *"Crisis, Contagion, and East Asian Stock Markets"*, World Scientific Publishing Co. and Centre for PBBEF Research, Vol.7, N°.1, pp. 119-151.

[131]   Yu, F. 2002.*"Accounting Transparency and the Term Structure of Credit Spreads"*, Working paper, University of California.

[132]   Zakoïan, J. M. 1994. *"Threshold Heteroskedastic Models"*, Journal of Economic Dynamics and Control, 18, pp. 931-955.

[133]   Zdravkovski, A. 2016. *"Stock market integration and diversification possibilities during financial crises: Evidence from Balkan countries"*, MPRA Paper No. 72182. Available at: https://mpra.ub.uni-muenchen.de/72182/.

[134]   Zhou, Ch. 2001. *"The term structure of credit spreads with jump risk"*. Journal of Banking and Finance ,No 11, pp. 2015-2040.

Appendixes
Appendix I

Appendix I. Graphs of capital dynamics and returns of the SEE indices

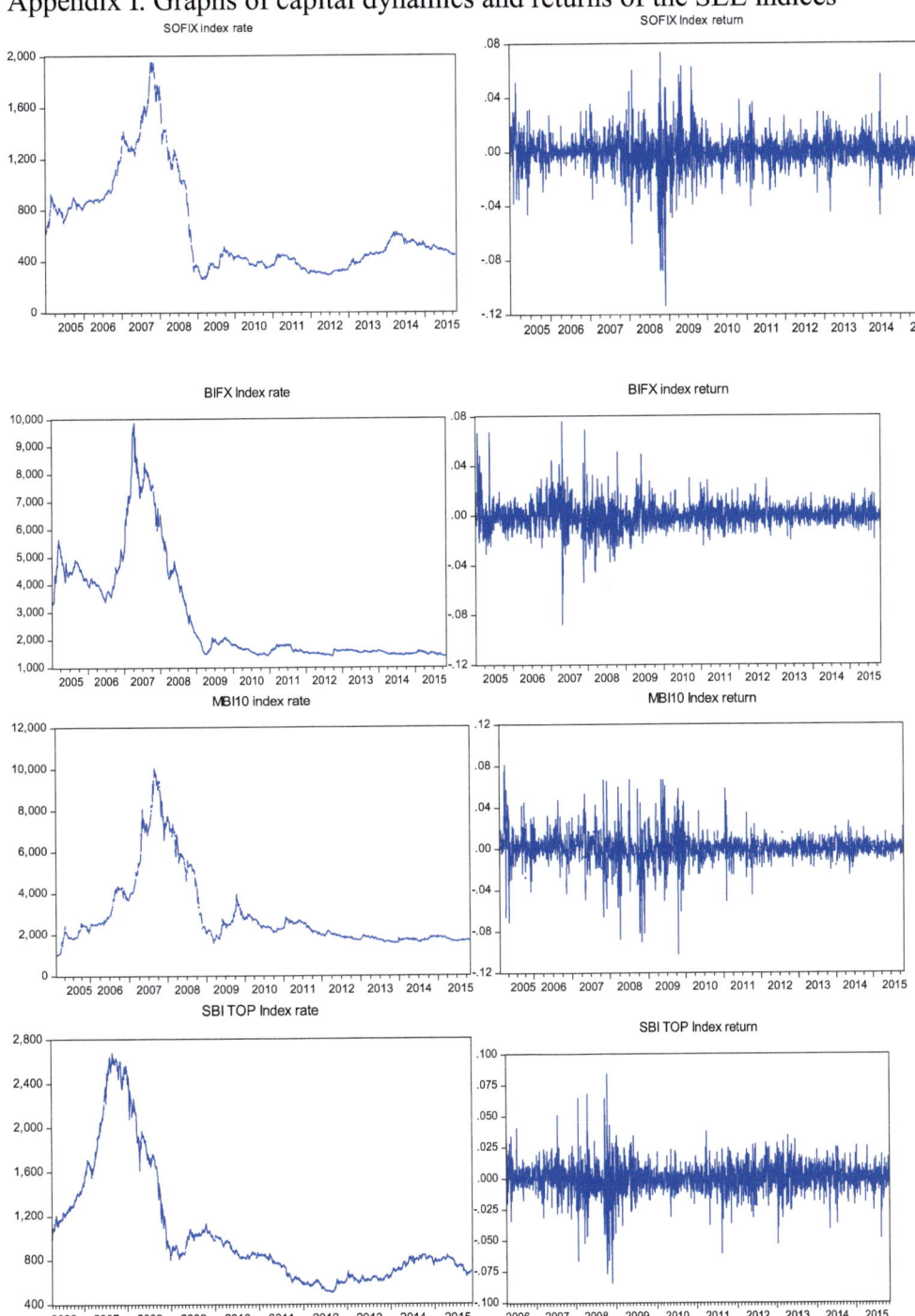

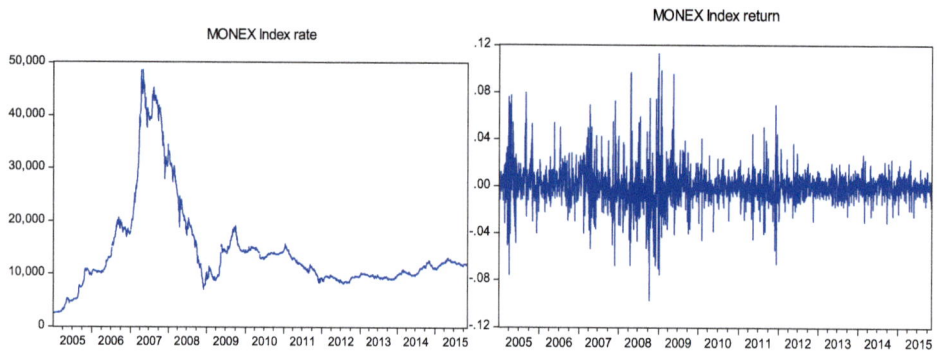
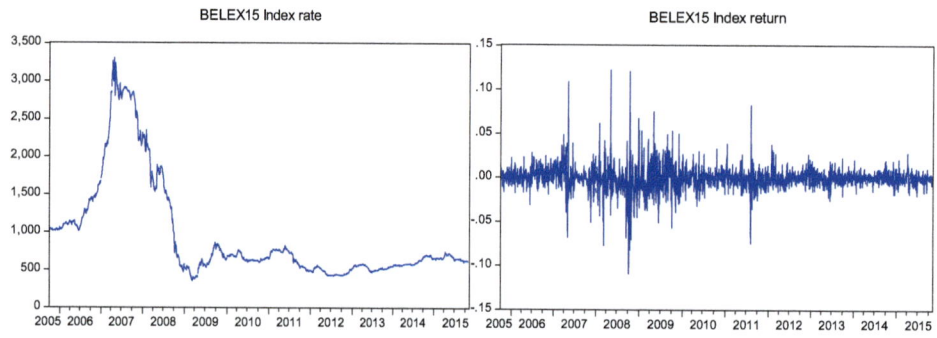
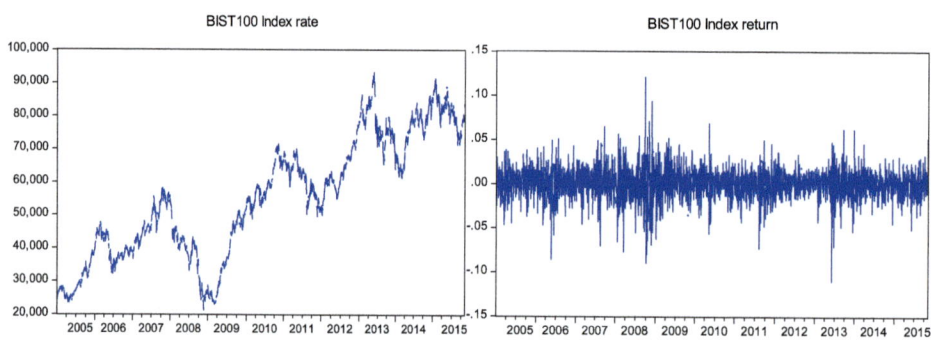
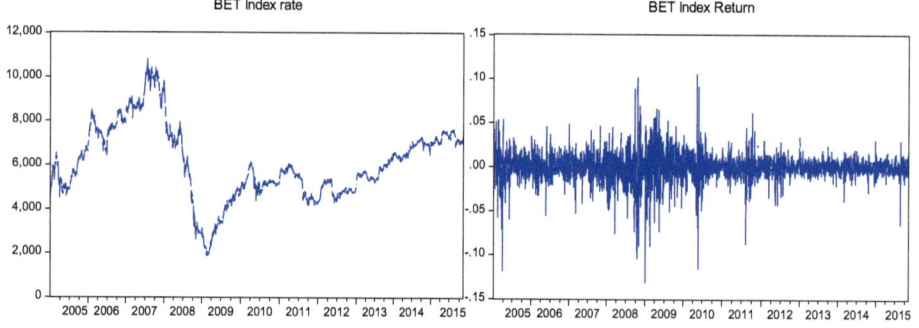

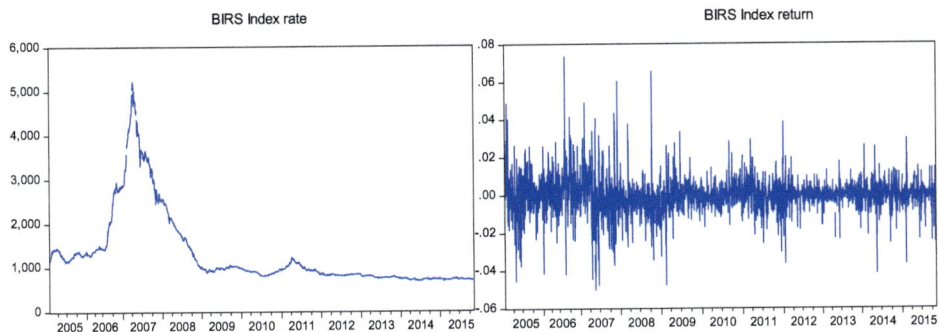
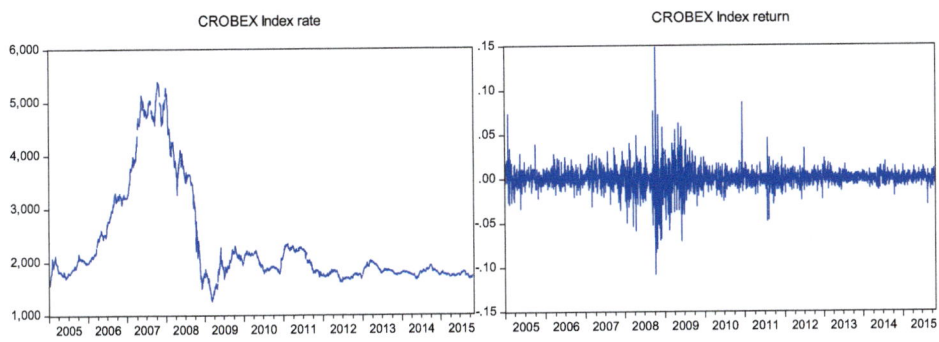
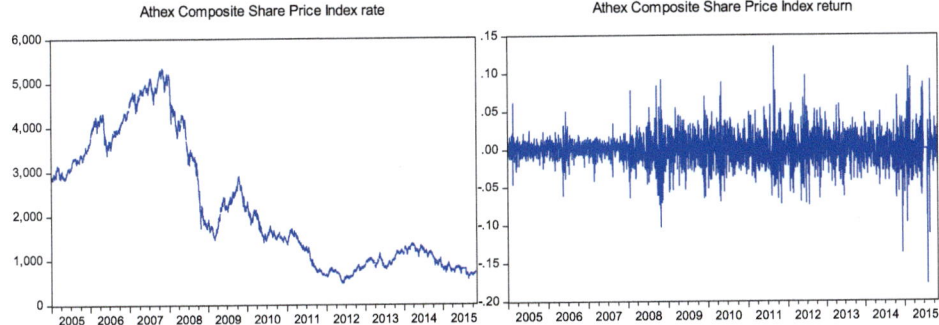

Appendix II. VAR Residual Heteroskedasticity Test

VAR Residual Heteroskedasticity Tests: No Cross Terms (only levels and squares)

Sample: 1 131
Included observations: 112

Joint test:

Chi-sq	df	Prob.
3238.960	2904	0.0000

Individual components:

Dependent	R-squared	$F(44,67)$	Prob.	Chi-sq(44)	Prob.
res1*res1	0.479496	1.402761	0.1042	53.70358	0.1499
res2*res2	0.612141	2.403251	0.0006	68.55976	0.0103
res3*res3	0.655472	2.897028	0.0000	73.41291	0.0035
res4*res4	0.520888	1.655504	0.0307	58.33950	0.0725
res5*res5	0.301398	0.656951	0.9303	33.75661	0.8682
res6*res6	0.615517	2.437726	0.0005	68.93790	0.0095
res7*res7	0.535280	1.753926	0.0186	59.95133	0.0549
res8*res8	0.593297	2.221351	0.0016	66.44928	0.0160
res9*res9	0.582667	2.125981	0.0026	65.25867	0.0203
res10*res10	0.341932	0.791208	0.7947	38.29636	0.7138
res11*res11	0.598496	2.269833	0.0012	67.03157	0.0142
res2*res1	0.479134	1.400726	0.1051	53.66302	0.1508
res3*res1	0.548678	1.851197	0.0112	61.45190	0.0420
res3*res2	0.663635	3.004288	0.0000	74.32717	0.0029
res4*res1	0.338355	0.778700	0.8104	37.89578	0.7296
res4*res2	0.555379	1.902050	0.0086	62.20246	0.0366
res4*res3	0.456578	1.279382	0.1790	51.13675	0.2138
res5*res1	0.444343	1.217681	0.2303	49.76640	0.2546
res5*res2	0.522049	1.663219	0.0296	58.46946	0.0709
res5*res3	0.519775	1.648136	0.0319	58.21482	0.0740
res5*res4	0.659973	2.955531	0.0000	73.91701	0.0032
res6*res1	0.578361	2.088717	0.0032	64.77638	0.0223
res6*res2	0.553320	1.886260	0.0093	61.97181	0.0381
res6*res3	0.651282	2.843911	0.0001	72.94354	0.0039
res6*res4	0.412031	1.067079	0.3994	46.14742	0.3836
res6*res5	0.473062	1.367037	0.1224	52.98292	0.1662
res7*res1	0.477210	1.389968	0.1104	53.44754	0.1556
res7*res2	0.628323	2.574179	0.0002	70.37214	0.0070
res7*res3	0.614910	2.431488	0.0005	68.86996	0.0097
res7*res4	0.556625	1.911671	0.0081	62.34197	0.0356
res7*res5	0.482682	1.420774	0.0959	54.06035	0.1423
res7*res6	0.596953	2.255316	0.0013	66.85879	0.0147
res8*res1	0.456150	1.277174	0.1806	51.08876	0.2151
res8*res2	0.539420	1.783378	0.0160	60.41500	0.0506
res8*res3	0.559251	1.932138	0.0073	62.63614	0.0337
res8*res4	0.603332	2.316073	0.0009	67.57324	0.0127
res8*res5	0.480149	1.406434	0.1024	53.77669	0.1483

res8*res6	0.419860	1.102029	0.3547	47.02427	0.3497
res8*res7	0.583528	2.133528	0.0025	65.35516	0.0199
res9*res1	0.480991	1.411183	0.1002	53.87095	0.1463
res9*res2	0.582047	2.120573	0.0027	65.18930	0.0206
res9*res3	0.538872	1.779448	0.0163	60.35361	0.0511
res9*res4	0.636896	2.670917	0.0001	71.33240	0.0057
res9*res5	0.368138	0.887178	0.6603	41.23148	0.5910
res9*res6	0.502077	1.535431	0.0557	56.23263	0.1022
res9*res7	0.609830	2.379996	0.0007	68.30091	0.0109
res9*res8	0.565154	1.979037	0.0057	63.29728	0.0297
res10*res1	0.379975	0.933185	0.5914	42.55718	0.5335
res10*res2	0.609346	2.375163	0.0007	68.24673	0.0110
res10*res3	0.648180	2.805420	0.0001	72.59620	0.0043
res10*res4	0.463047	1.313140	0.1550	51.86126	0.1941
res10*res5	0.729403	4.104554	0.0000	81.69310	0.0005
res10*res6	0.551965	1.875950	0.0098	61.82005	0.0392
res10*res7	0.604597	2.328346	0.0009	67.71482	0.0123
res10*res8	0.565603	1.982656	0.0056	63.34756	0.0295
res10*res9	0.534403	1.747755	0.0192	59.85311	0.0559
res11*res1	0.643323	2.746474	0.0001	72.05214	0.0048
res11*res2	0.608855	2.370271	0.0007	68.19175	0.0112
res11*res3	0.687451	3.349228	0.0000	76.99446	0.0015
res11*res4	0.496576	1.502016	0.0654	55.61655	0.1125
res11*res5	0.414186	1.076610	0.3869	46.38886	0.3741
res11*res6	0.636431	2.665544	0.0001	71.28023	0.0057
res11*res7	0.665806	3.033688	0.0000	74.57025	0.0027
res11*res8	0.604174	2.324233	0.0009	67.66747	0.0124
res11*res9	0.635489	2.654726	0.0002	71.17478	0.0059
res11*res10	0.588700	2.179505	0.0019	65.93443	0.0177

Appendix III. VAR

Residual Normality Test
VAR Residual Normality Tests
Orthogonalization: Cholesky (Lutkepohl)
Null Hypothesis: residuals are multivariate normal
Date: 07/12/18   Time: 23:41
Sample: 1 131
Included observations: 112

Component	Skewness	Chi-sq	df	Prob.
1	0.020208	0.007623	1	0.9304
2	-0.061893	0.071508	1	0.7892
3	0.294321	1.616992	1	0.2035
4	0.630592	7.422720	1	0.0064
5	1.182736	26.11215	1	0.0000
6	0.019470	0.007076	1	0.9330
7	0.092314	0.159076	1	0.6900
8	0.231360	0.999176	1	0.3175
9	-0.087757	0.143758	1	0.7046
10	0.229111	0.979852	1	0.3222
11	-0.021781	0.008856	1	0.9250
Joint		37.52879	11	0.0001

Component	Kurtosis	Chi-sq	df	Prob.
1	3.180178	0.151500	1	0.6971
2	2.881839	0.065156	1	0.7985
3	3.495285	1.144769	1	0.2846
4	3.762147	2.710718	1	0.0997
5	8.273629	129.7854	1	0.0000
6	3.161110	0.121130	1	0.7278
7	3.800355	2.989316	1	0.0838
8	2.874548	0.073445	1	0.7864
9	2.682419	0.470670	1	0.4927
10	3.483259	1.089852	1	0.2965
11	3.079431	0.029443	1	0.8638
Joint		138.6314	11	0.0000

Component	Jarque-Bera	df	Prob.
1	0.159122	2	0.9235
2	0.136664	2	0.9340
3	2.761760	2	0.2514
4	10.13344	2	0.0063
5	155.8976	2	0.0000
6	0.128207	2	0.9379
7	3.148392	2	0.2072
8	1.072620	2	0.5849
9	0.614428	2	0.7355
10	2.069704	2	0.3553
11	0.038299	2	0.9810

| | Joint | 176.1602 | 22 | 0.0000 | | | | | | |

Appendix IV. Vector Autoregression Estimates

Vector Autoregression Estimates												
Sample (adjusted): 20 131												
Included observations: 112 after adjustments												
Standard errors in ( ) & t-statistics in()												
	RATHEX	RBELEX	RBET	RBIFX	RBIRS	RBIST	RCROBEX	RMBI	RMONEX	RSBITOP	RSOFIX
RATHEX(-1)	-0.026322	0.052253	0.002605	0.032780	-0.071302	-0.184099	-0.030899	-0.108695	-0.008568	-0.028621	0.069942
	(0.13990)	(0.09758)	(0.11816)	(0.08060)	(0.07942)	(0.10316)	(0.09360)	(0.11158)	(0.12891)	(0.07496)	(0.11474)
	[-0.18815]	[0.53548]	[0.02204]	[0.40668]	[-0.89776]	[-1.78456]	[-0.33012]	[-0.97415]	[-0.06647]	[-0.38179]	[0.60954]
RATHEX(-2)	-0.021280	-0.034384	-0.075185	-0.009941	0.047860	-0.006505	-0.032893	-0.185342	-0.145096	-0.001291	-0.042012
	(0.13928)	(0.09715)	(0.11764)	(0.08025)	(0.07907)	(0.10271)	(0.09319)	(0.11109)	(0.12835)	(0.07464)	(0.11424)
	[-0.15278]	[-0.35391]	[-0.63913]	[-0.12388]	[0.60525]	[-0.06333]	[-0.35298]	[-1.66841]	[-1.13049]	[-0.01730]	[-0.36775]
RBELEX(-1)	0.323684	0.086425	0.116405	-0.052599	0.148307	0.407745	0.334771	0.518937	0.263905	0.084303	0.150271
	(0.23793)	(0.16596)	(0.20095)	(0.13709)	(0.13508)	(0.17545)	(0.15919)	(0.18977)	(0.21925)	(0.12750)	(0.19515)
	[1.36041]	[0.52075]	[0.57926]	[-0.38369]	[1.09793]	[2.32395]	[2.10301]	[2.73459]	[1.20367]	[0.66122]	[0.77002]
RBELEX(-2)	-0.100587	-0.250887	0.041658	-0.170564	-0.038431	0.129357	-0.063175	0.013844	-0.166661	0.032571	-0.126927
	(0.20233)	(0.14113)	(0.17088)	(0.11657)	(0.11487)	(0.14920)	(0.13537)	(0.16137)	(0.18644)	(0.10842)	(0.16595)
	[-0.49715]	[-1.77773]	[0.24378]	[-1.46315]	[-0.33458]	[0.86701]	[-0.46670]	[0.08579]	[-0.89390]	[0.30042]	[-0.76485]
RBET(-1)	-0.053545	0.473961	0.285687	0.218055	0.302230	0.453580	0.326690	0.071138	0.386703	0.084117	0.266135
	(0.19744)	(0.13772)	(0.16675)	(0.11376)	(0.11209)	(0.14559)	(0.13210)	(0.15747)	(0.18194)	(0.10580)	(0.16194)
	[-0.27119]	[3.44153]	[1.71323]	[1.91685]	[2.69630]	[3.11536]	[2.47312]	[0.45175]	[2.12547]	[0.79507]	[1.64341]
RBET(-2)	-0.122022	0.124473	-0.065684	0.107645	-0.104114	-0.090801	0.023173	0.085293	0.365236	0.068477	-0.039371
	(0.21636)	(0.15092)	(0.18273)	(0.12466)	(0.12283)	(0.15955)	(0.14475)	(0.17256)	(0.19937)	(0.11594)	(0.17746)
	[-0.56398]	[0.82479]	[-0.35945]	[0.86352]	[-0.84761]	[-0.56912]	[0.16008]	[0.49427]	[1.83192]	[0.59063]	[-0.22186]
RBIFX(-1)	-0.380006	0.171469	0.077542	-0.161263	0.135697	-0.426432	-0.325735	0.146720	-0.086845	-0.142859	-0.158005
	(0.21563)	(0.15041)	(0.18212)	(0.12424)	(0.12242)	(0.15901)	(0.14427)	(0.17198)	(0.19870)	(0.11555)	(0.17686)
	[-1.76229]	[1.14004]	[0.42578]	[-1.29802]	[1.10847]	[-2.68181]	[-2.25786]	[0.85312]	[-0.43706]	[-1.23638]	[-0.89338]
RBIFX(-2)	-0.054996	0.134015	-0.295301	0.161228	-0.215057	-0.216761	-0.034456	-0.230156	0.102492	-0.034248	-0.060267
	(0.21848)	(0.15239)	(0.18452)	(0.12588)	(0.12403)	(0.16111)	(0.14617)	(0.17425)	(0.20132)	(0.11707)	(0.17920)
	[-0.25172]	[0.87941]	[-1.60035]	[1.28082]	[-1.73385]	[-1.34543]	[-0.23572]	[-1.32082]	[0.50909]	[-0.29254]	[-0.33632]
RBIRS(-1)	0.200357	0.388722	0.239272	0.667351	0.409500	0.210293	0.355139	0.169156	0.396961	0.154581	0.168595
	(0.19538)	(0.13628)	(0.16502)	(0.11257)	(0.11092)	(0.14408)	(0.13072)	(0.15583)	(0.18004)	(0.10470)	(0.16025)
	[1.02545]	[2.85228]	[1.44998]	[5.92818]	[3.69173]	[1.45957]	[2.71677]	[1.08549]	[2.20480]	[1.47645]	[1.05204]
RBIRS(-2)	0.229395	0.067426	-0.052092	-0.048111	0.046033	0.054237	0.056236	-0.220131	-0.049894	0.007567	0.167058
	(0.21555)	(0.15035)	(0.18205)	(0.12419)	(0.12237)	(0.15895)	(0.14421)	(0.17192)	(0.19863)	(0.11550)	(0.17679)
	[1.06423]	[0.44846]	[-0.28614]	[-0.38739]	[0.37617]	[0.34122]	[0.38995]	[-1.28045]	[-0.25120]	[0.06551]	[0.94492]
RBIST(-1)	0.217779	0.127383	0.110761	0.047063	-0.083191	0.014198	0.137651	0.099107	-0.054267	0.101174	0.117126
	(0.16272)	(0.11350)	(0.13743)	(0.09375)	(0.09238)	(0.11999)	(0.10887)	(0.12978)	(0.14995)	(0.08720)	(0.13347)
	[1.33835]	[1.12230]	[0.80593]	[0.50198]	[-0.90052]	[0.11832]	[1.26438]	[0.76364]	[-0.36191]	[1.16031]	[0.87757]
RBIST(-2)	-0.221164	-0.233826	-0.049555	-0.090545	-0.111186	-0.073452	-0.091627	-0.192153	-0.227541	-0.047190	-0.116047
	(0.15416)	(0.10753)	(0.13020)	(0.08882)	(0.08752)	(0.11368)	(0.10314)	(0.12296)	(0.14206)	(0.08261)	(0.12644)
	[-1.43461]	[-2.17449]	[-0.38059]	[-1.01939]	[-1.27038]	[-0.64612]	[-0.88835]	[-1.56278]	[-1.60174]	[-0.57125]	[-0.91777]
RCROBEX(-1)	-0.464018	-0.152658	-0.549878	0.015956	-0.210142	-0.702266	-0.616882	-0.149951	-0.352375	-0.174135	-0.422920
	(0.23300)	(0.16252)	(0.19679)	(0.13425)	(0.13228)	(0.17182)	(0.15589)	(0.18584)	(0.21471)	(0.12485)	(0.19111)
	[-1.99148]	[-0.93930]	[-2.79426]	[0.11886]	[-1.58862]	[-4.08727]	[-3.95721]	[-0.80690]	[-1.64119]	[-1.39470]	[-2.21299]
RCROBEX(-2)	0.069457	0.143975	-0.106570	0.141298	0.186965	-0.155751	0.016695	0.055390	0.075433	-0.047368	-0.014112
	(0.23194)	(0.16178)	(0.19589)	(0.13364)	(0.13168)	(0.17104)	(0.15518)	(0.18499)	(0.21373)	(0.12429)	(0.19024)
	[0.29946]	[0.88992]	[-0.54402]	[1.05734]	[1.41987]	[-0.91063]	[0.10759]	[0.29942]	[0.35293]	[-0.38112]	[-0.07418]

RMBI(-1)	-0.004463	**-0.271097**	-0.045527	-0.162121	-0.140378	-0.214453	-0.099831	**-0.282792**	-0.290358	-0.114594	0.141078
	(0.17337)	**(0.12093)**	(0.14643)	(0.09989)	(0.09843)	(0.12785)	(0.11599)	**(0.13828)**	(0.15976)	(0.09290)	(0.14220)
	[-0.02574]	**[-2.24175]**	[-0.31092]	[-1.62299]	[-1.42621]	[-1.67741]	[-0.86066]	**[-2.04510]**	[-1.81746]	[-1.23348]	[0.99210]
RMBI(-2)	0.086289	-0.094208	0.196319	-0.048926	-0.090515	0.205558	0.107874	-0.053427	-0.115995	0.056119	0.106386
	(0.17177)	(0.11981)	(0.14507)	(0.09897)	(0.09752)	(0.12666)	(0.11492)	(0.13700)	(0.15828)	(0.09204)	(0.14088)
	[0.50236]	[-0.78630]	[1.35325]	[-0.49437]	[-0.92820]	[1.62286]	[0.93868]	[-0.38999]	[-0.73284]	[0.60970]	[0.75513]
RMONEX(-1)	0.143509	0.164547	-0.050967	-0.027902	0.133039	0.233098	0.085084	0.149525	**0.311316**	0.172478	-0.103074
	(0.16697)	(0.11646)	(0.14102)	(0.09620)	(0.09479)	(0.12313)	(0.11171)	(0.13317)	**(0.15386)**	(0.08947)	(0.13695)
	[0.85949]	[1.41285]	[-0.36142]	[-0.29004]	[1.40349]	[1.89318]	[0.76166]	[1.12282]	**[2.02337]**	[1.92775]	[-0.75265]
RMONEX(-2)	-0.162402	-0.021784	0.122029	-0.080475	0.004713	-0.089296	-0.076470	0.100109	-0.111451	-0.011100	-0.008514
	(0.17427)	(0.12155)	(0.14718)	(0.10041)	(0.09893)	(0.12851)	(0.11659)	(0.13899)	(0.16058)	(0.09338)	(0.14293)
	[-0.93192]	[-0.17921]	[0.82910]	[-0.80150]	[0.04764]	[-0.69488]	[-0.65588]	[0.72026]	[-0.69404]	[-0.11887]	[-0.05957]
RSBITOP(-1)	0.110616	0.006689	0.151752	-0.014310	-0.029075	0.007539	0.129033	0.153262	0.071961	0.112005	0.382414
	(0.25029)	(0.17458)	(0.21139)	(0.14421)	(0.14209)	(0.18456)	(0.16745)	(0.19962)	(0.23064)	(0.13412)	(0.20529)
	[0.44196]	[0.03832]	[0.71789]	[-0.09923]	[-0.20462]	[0.04085]	[0.77056]	[0.76776]	[0.31201]	[0.83513]	[1.86284]
RSBITOP(-2)	0.163312	**0.391150**	0.145808	0.110917	0.169039	0.225895	0.152867	**0.466434**	**0.643550**	0.082414	0.225324
	(0.24613)	**(0.17168)**	(0.20788)	(0.14181)	(0.13974)	(0.18150)	(0.16467)	**(0.19631)**	**(0.22681)**	(0.13189)	(0.20188)
	[0.66351]	**[2.27832]**	[0.70140]	[0.78213]	[1.20971]	[1.24459]	[0.92829]	**[2.37601]**	**[2.83741]**	[0.62486]	[1.11613]
RSOFIX(-1)	0.329405	0.055312	0.121357	0.046627	0.021675	-0.021315	**0.337739**	0.173006	0.087185	0.116827	0.134873
	(0.17677)	(0.12330)	(0.14930)	(0.10185)	(0.10036)	(0.13035)	**(0.11827)**	(0.14099)	(0.16289)	(0.09472)	(0.14499)
	[1.86346]	[0.44859]	[0.81286]	[0.45781]	[0.21598]	[-0.16351]	**[2.85573]**	[1.22711]	[0.53524]	[1.23335]	[0.93024]
RSOFIX(-2)	0.070987	-0.077482	0.094587	0.199185	0.079197	**0.314839**	-0.109989	-0.105319	-0.296682	0.080113	0.056546
	(0.17650)	(0.12311)	(0.14907)	(0.10169)	(0.10020)	**(0.13016)**	(0.11809)	(0.14077)	(0.16264)	(0.09458)	(0.14477)
	[0.40219]	[-0.62935]	[0.63451]	[1.95867]	[0.79036]	**[2.41895]**	[-0.93141]	[-0.74815]	[-1.82411]	[0.84704]	[0.39060]
C	-0.012797	0.000845	-0.000819	-0.003230	-0.002888	0.003588	-0.003756	-0.006091	0.000354	-0.004304	-0.002174
	(0.01032)	(0.00720)	(0.00872)	(0.00595)	(0.00586)	(0.00761)	(0.00690)	(0.00823)	(0.00951)	(0.00553)	(0.00846)
	[-1.24007]	[0.11737]	[-0.09391]	[-0.54329]	[-0.49302]	[0.47154]	[-0.54406]	[-0.74004]	[0.03726]	[-0.77833]	[-0.25679]
R-squared	0.222431	0.598312	0.283591	0.529276	0.464348	0.365868	0.520079	0.462358	0.439513	0.362875	0.385082
Adj. R-squared	0.030223	0.499018	0.106502	0.412918	0.331940	0.209116	0.401447	0.329458	0.300966	0.205384	0.233080
Sum sq. resids	0.883361	0.429783	0.630115	0.293240	0.284712	0.480350	0.395410	0.561924	0.750091	0.253648	0.594264
S.E. equation	0.099626	0.069491	0.084142	0.057401	0.056560	0.073466	0.066654	0.079459	0.091804	0.053385	0.081714
F-statistic	1.157241	6.025682	2.601400	4.548663	3.506940	2.334061	4.383961	3.478985	3.172298	2.304095	2.533397
Log likelihood	112.2600	152.6054	131.1785	174.0135	175.6662	146.3762	157.2734	137.5926	121.4182	182.1360	134.4590
Akaike AIC	-1.593928	-2.314381	-1.931760	-2.696670	-2.726183	-2.203147	-2.397739	-2.046296	-1.757468	-2.841715	-1.990339
Schwarz SC	-1.035665	-1.756118	-1.373497	-2.138407	-2.167920	-1.644884	-1.839476	-1.488033	-1.199205	-2.283452	-1.432075
Mean dependent	-0.014563	-0.004678	-7.00E-06	-0.008298	-0.006420	0.007668	-0.003931	-0.004602	-0.001069	-0.004749	-0.006153
S.D. dependent	0.101167	0.098179	0.089016	0.074915	0.069199	0.082609	0.086154	0.097036	0.109803	0.059888	0.093308
Determinant resid covariance (dof adj.)	5.50E-28										
Determinant resid covariance	4.38E-29										
Log likelihood	1908.492										
Akaike information criterion	-29.56236										
Schwarz criterion	-23.42146										

RATHEX = - 0.0263216621453*RATHEX(-1) - 0.0212797696839*RATHEX(-2) + 0.323684138118*RBELEX(-1) - 0.100587390452*RBELEX(-2) - 0.0535446989417*RBET(-1) - 0.122022494308*RBET(-2) - 0.380005854374*RBIFX(-1) - 0.0549958348217*RBIFX(-2) + 0.200356955916*RBIRS(-1) + 0.229394973451*RBIRS(-2) + 0.217779349583*RBIST(-1) - 0.22116428629*RBIST(-2) - 0.464017910874*RCROBEX(-1) + 0.0694567540322*RCROBEX(-2) - 0.00446261610532*RMBI(-1) + 0.0862888417865*RMBI(-2) + 0.143508593222*RMONEX(-1) - 0.162401950271*RMONEX(-2) + 0.110616269893*RSBITOP(-1) + 0.163311931272*RSBITOP(-2) + 0.329404925303*RSOFIX(-1) + 0.0709869967509*RSOFIX(-2) - 0.0127971185295

RBELEX = 0.0522525334972*RATHEX(-1) - 0.0343837287846*RATHEX(-2) + 0.0864254634225*RBELEX(-1) - 0.25088691389*RBELEX(-2) + 0.473960812779*RBET(-1) + 0.124473115471*RBET(-2) + 0.171469186748*RBIFX(-1) + 0.134015181177*RBIFX(-2) + 0.388721722109*RBIRS(-1) + 0.0674263031318*RBIRS(-2) + 0.127382936239*RBIST(-1) - 0.233826040939*RBIST(-2) - 0.152657764943*RCROBEX(-1) + 0.143974766801*RCROBEX(-2) - 0.271097207214*RMBI(-1) - 0.0942081048915*RMBI(-2) + 0.164547075258*RMONEX(-1) - 0.0217840655767*RMONEX(-2) + 0.00668949327623*RSBITOP(-1) + 0.39115004995*RSBITOP(-2) + 0.0553115169533*RSOFIX(-1) - 0.0774820658714*RSOFIX(-2) + 0.000844830955063

RBET = 0.00260462443865*RATHEX(-1) - 0.0751848988034*RATHEX(-2) + 0.116404606536*RBELEX(-1) + 0.0416584583062*RBELEX(-2) + 0.285687324341*RBET(-1) - 0.0656842546342*RBET(-2) + 0.0775415068477*RBIFX(-1) - 0.295300635024*RBIFX(-2) + 0.23927231827*RBIRS(-1) - 0.0520915811739*RBIRS(-2) + 0.110760954192*RBIST(-1) - 0.0495546249046*RBIST(-2) - 0.549878016082*RCROBEX(-1) - 0.106569702718*RCROBEX(-2) - 0.0455267989019*RMBI(-1) + 0.19631910125*RMBI(-2) - 0.0509667474335*RMONEX(-1) + 0.122029134192*RMONEX(-2) + 0.151752415902*RSBITOP(-1) + 0.145807821012*RSBITOP(-2) + 0.121357135397*RSOFIX(-1) + 0.0945868696887*RSOFIX(-2) - 0.000818513461578

RBIFX = 0.032780230549*RATHEX(-1) - 0.00994129857728*RATHEX(-2) - 0.0525992871923*RBELEX(-1) - 0.170564220576*RBELEX(-2) + 0.218055120064*RBET(-1) + 0.107645041294*RBET(-2) - 0.161263015027*RBIFX(-1) + 0.161227528*RBIFX(-2) + 0.667350862928*RBIRS(-1) - 0.048110745484*RBIRS(-2) + 0.047062917947*RBIST(-1) - 0.0905448263111*RBIST(-2) + 0.0159558758262*RCROBEX(-1) + 0.141298008946*RCROBEX(-2) - 0.162121132718*RMBI(-1) - 0.0489255226255*RMBI(-2) - 0.0279021991801*RMONEX(-1) - 0.0804748313922*RMONEX(-2) - 0.0143097610062*RSBITOP(-1) + 0.110916510891*RSBITOP(-2) + 0.0466273842578*RSOFIX(-1) + 0.199184502108*RSOFIX(-2) - 0.00323026622536

RBIRS = - 0.0713023056057*RATHEX(-1) + 0.0478599554128*RATHEX(-2) + 0.148307269381*RBELEX(-1) - 0.0384312261356*RBELEX(-2) + 0.302230395196*RBET(-1) - 0.104114316729*RBET(-2) + 0.135696682903*RBIFX(-1) - 0.215057119463*RBIFX(-2) + 0.409499926761*RBIRS(-1) + 0.0460327977999*RBIRS(-2) - 0.0831906488178*RBIST(-1) - 0.111185895547*RBIST(-2) - 0.210141526869*RCROBEX(-1) + 0.186964844517*RCROBEX(-2) - 0.140377687097*RMBI(-1) - 0.090515079679*RMBI(-2) + 0.133039476339*RMONEX(-1) + 0.00471311540126*RMONEX(-2) - 0.0290747044313*RSBITOP(-1) + 0.169039129944*RSBITOP(-2) + 0.0216750278955*RSOFIX(-1) + 0.0791968510245*RSOFIX(-2) - 0.00288845487464

RBIST = - 0.184099317175*RATHEX(-1) - 0.00650469916287*RATHEX(-2) + 0.407745403603*RBELEX(-1) + 0.129356793573*RBELEX(-2) + 0.453579606326*RBET(-1) - 0.0908008631332*RBET(-2) - 0.426432472694*RBIFX(-1) - 0.216760566923*RBIFX(-2) + 0.21029311594*RBIRS(-1) + 0.0542366988783*RBIRS(-2) + 0.0141976890834*RBIST(-1) - 0.073452167214*RBIST(-2) - 0.702266127131*RCROBEX(-1) - 0.155750738052*RCROBEX(-2) - 0.214452798217*RMBI(-1) + 0.205557773608*RMBI(-2) + 0.233098162562*RMONEX(-1) - 0.0892960350371*RMONEX(-2) + 0.0075387173335*RSBITOP(-1) + 0.225895185144*RSBITOP(-2) - 0.0213145696017*RSOFIX(-1) + 0.314838786493*RSOFIX(-2) + 0.00358836259155

RCROBEX = - 0.0308989378931*RATHEX(-1) - 0.0328931287767*RATHEX(-2) + 0.334771462178*RBELEX(-1) - 0.0631751650499*RBELEX(-2) + 0.326689780069*RBET(-1) + 0.0231729593935*RBET(-2) - 0.325734775979*RBIFX(-1) - 0.0344561818205*RBIFX(-2) + 0.355138591845*RBIRS(-1) + 0.0562362986438*RBIRS(-2) + 0.137650762101*RBIST(-1) - 0.0916266893262*RBIST(-2) - 0.61688246088*RCROBEX(-1) + 0.0166949604*RCROBEX(-2) - 0.0998312345802*RMBI(-1) + 0.107874119291*RMBI(-2) + 0.0850844311691*RMONEX(-1) - 0.0764701223229*RMONEX(-2) + 0.129033260663*RSBITOP(-1) + 0.152866714429*RSBITOP(-2) + 0.337738881253*RSOFIX(-1) - 0.10998864498*RSOFIX(-2) - 0.00375633414038

RMBI = - 0.108694730534*RATHEX(-1) - 0.18534222961*RATHEX(-2) + 0.518936899068*RBELEX(-1) + 0.0138436293611*RBELEX(-2) + 0.0711384292522*RBET(-1) + 0.0852925289345*RBET(-2) + 0.146720045432*RBIFX(-1) - 0.230155826968*RBIFX(-2) + 0.16915554714*RBIRS(-1) - 0.220130675661*RBIRS(-2) + 0.0991072105512*RBIST(-1) - 0.192153338206*RBIST(-2) - 0.14995129421*RCROBEX(-1) + 0.0553896402624*RCROBEX(-2) - 0.282791799102*RMBI(-1) - 0.0534274463213*RMBI(-2) + 0.149525457131*RMONEX(-1) + 0.100109210997*RMONEX(-2) + 0.15326168324*RSBITOP(-1) + 0.466434104467*RSBITOP(-2) + 0.173006295139*RSOFIX(-1) - 0.105319266105*RSOFIX(-2) - 0.00609106260579

RMONEX = - 0.00856836742722*RATHEX(-1) - 0.145096066683*RATHEX(-2) + 0.263904857057*RBELEX(-1) - 0.166660768014*RBELEX(-2) + 0.386703074895*RBET(-1) + 0.365236394876*RBET(-2) - 0.0868449872346*RBIFX(-1) + 0.102492332608*RBIFX(-2) + 0.396960581016*RBIRS(-1) - 0.049894159461*RBIRS(-2) - 0.0542671953618*RBIST(-1) - 0.227541138383*RBIST(-2) - 0.352375131947*RCROBEX(-1) + 0.0754328674747*RCROBEX(-2) - 0.290358460293*RMBI(-1) - 0.115995011487*RMBI(-2) + 0.311315835154*RMONEX(-1) - 0.111450936935*RMONEX(-2) + 0.0719606872781*RSBITOP(-1) + 0.643550150922*RSBITOP(-2) + 0.0871854633383*RSOFIX(-1) - 0.296681954515*RSOFIX(-2) + 0.000354328969038

RSBITOP = - 0.0286211013562*RATHEX(-1) - 0.00129143267591*RATHEX(-2) + 0.0843028666888*RBELEX(-1) + 0.0325713851903*RBELEX(-2) + 0.0841173526929*RBET(-1) + 0.0684765381217*RBET(-2) - 0.14285931896*RBIFX(-1) - 0.0342482903283*RBIFX(-2) + 0.154581078047*RBIRS(-1) + 0.00756680511657*RBIRS(-2) + 0.101173645445*RBIST(-1) - 0.0471902302294*RBIST(-2) - 0.174134592252*RCROBEX(-1) - 0.0473679890014*RCROBEX(-2) - 0.114593718485*RMBI(-1) + 0.0561189654928*RMBI(-2) + 0.172477956391*RMONEX(-1) - 0.0110998702278*RMONEX(-2) + 0.11200489328*RSBITOP(-1) + 0.0824138890657*RSBITOP(-2) + 0.116827243527*RSOFIX(-1) + 0.0801126499481*RSOFIX(-2) - 0.00430406709793

RSOFIX = 0.0699417779094*RATHEX(-1) - 0.042012468341*RATHEX(-2) + 0.150270797152*RBELEX(-1) - 0.126927137503*RBELEX(-2) + 0.2661350387*RBET(-1) - 0.0393713205467*RBET(-2) - 0.158004899514*RBIFX(-1) - 0.0602673526211*RBIFX(-2) + 0.168595111597*RBIRS(-1) + 0.167057500673*RBIRS(-2) + 0.11712558886*RBIST(-1) - 0.116047351909*RBIST(-2) - 0.422919608065*RCROBEX(-1) - 0.0141116659714*RCROBEX(-2) + 0.141078120951*RMBI(-1) + 0.106386012568*RMBI(-2) - 0.103073981435*RMONEX(-1) - 0.00851439681808*RMONEX(-2) + 0.382414115988*RSBITOP(-1) + 0.22532445293*RSBITOP(-2) + 0.134873310843*RSOFIX(-1) + 0.0565464762179*RSOFIX(-2) - 0.002173510032

Appendix V. Impulse Response Function Results

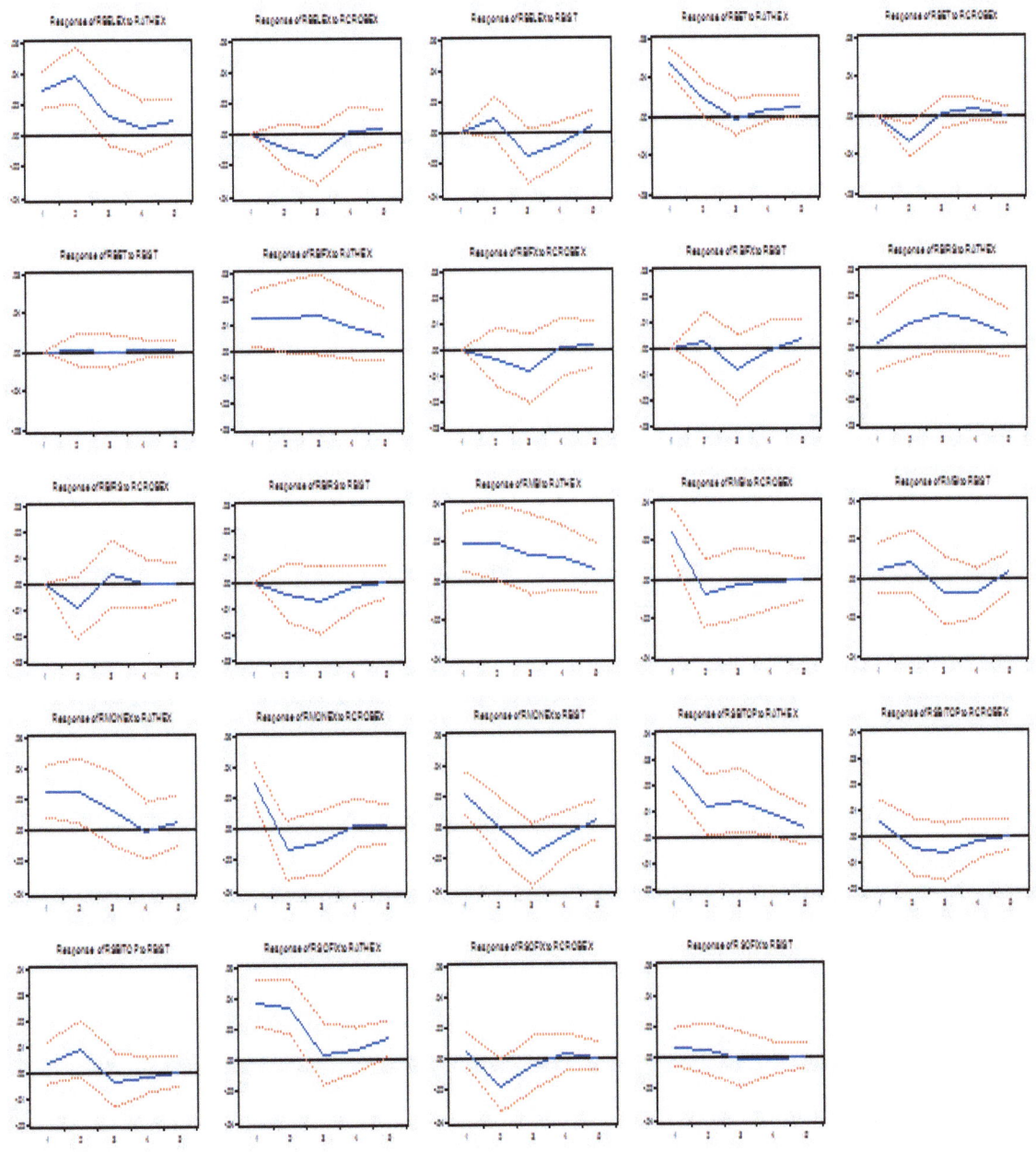

Appendix VI. Results from panel unit root test: Summary for the first differences of the explored variables

DCash				
Method	Statistic	Probability	Cross- sections	Observations
Null: Unit Root (assumes common unit root process)				
Levin, Lin & Chu	-16.4345	0.0000	20	578
Null: Unit Root (assumes individual unit root process)				
Im, Pesaran & Shin W- Stat	-20.4358	0.0000	20	578
ADF- Fisher Chi-square	386.784	0.0000	20	578
PP- Fisher Chi-square	545.087	0.0000	20	598

DCDS				
Method	Statistic	Probability	Cross- sections	Observations
Null: Unit Root (assumes common unit root process)				
Levin, Lin & Chu	-7.46616	0.0000	20	580
Null: Unit Root (assumes individual unit root process)				
Im, Pesaran & Shin W- Stat	-9.55432	0.0000	20	580
ADF- Fisher Chi-square	164.677	0.0000	20	580
PP- Fisher Chi-square	379.627	0.0000	20	600

DCurrent				
Method	Statistic	Probability	Cross- sections	Observations
Null: Unit Root (assumes common unit root process)				
Levin, Lin & Chu	-17.0221	0.0000	20	578
Null: Unit Root (assumes individual unit root process)				
Im, Pesaran & Shin W- Stat	-21.2275	0.0000	20	578
ADF- Fisher Chi-square	401.821	0.0000	20	578
PP- Fisher Chi-square	527.329	0.0000	20	598

DEBIT				
Method	Statistic	Probability	Cross- sections	Observations
Null: Unit Root (assumes common unit root process)				
Levin, Lin & Chu	-13.3377	0.0000	18	504
Null: Unit Root (assumes individual unit root process)				
Im, Pesaran & Shin W- Stat	-17.6016	0.0000	18	504
ADF- Fisher Chi-square	318.128	0.0000	18	504
PP- Fisher Chi-square	427.727	0.0000	18	526

DINTWO				
Method	Statistic	Probability	Cross- sections	Observations
Null: Unit Root (assumes common unit root process)				
Levin, Lin & Chu	-10.7929	0.0000	6	172
Null: Unit Root (assumes individual unit root process)				
Im, Pesaran & Shin W- Stat	-11.1973	0.0000	6	172
ADF- Fisher Chi-square	116.903	0.0000	6	172
PP- Fisher Chi-square	175.441	0.0000	6	178

DLeverage				
Method	Statistic	Probability	Cross- sections	Observations
Null: Unit Root (assumes common unit root process)				
Levin, Lin & Chu	-11.8635	0.0000	19	549
Null: Unit Root (assumes individual unit root process)				
Im, Pesaran & Shin W- Stat	-16.4065	0.0000	19	549
ADF- Fisher Chi-square	303.691	0.0000	19	549
PP- Fisher Chi-square	484.670	0.0000	19	568

D Firm size				
Method	Statistic	Probability	Cross- sections	Observations
Null: Unit Root (assumes common unit root process)				
Levin, Lin & Chu	-15.2478	0.0000	20	578
Null: Unit Root (assumes individual unit root process)				
Im, Pesaran & Shin W- Stat	-17.8108	0.0000	20	578
ADF- Fisher Chi-square	288.165	0.0000	20	578
PP- Fisher Chi-square	462.625	0.0000	20	598

D RiskfreeRate				
Method	Statistic	Probability	Cross- sections	Observations
Null: Unit Root (assumes common unit root process)				
Levin, Lin & Chu	-3.48293	0.0002	20	580
Null: Unit Root (assumes individual unit root process)				
Im, Pesaran & Shin W- Stat	-8.16261	0.0000	20	580
ADF- Fisher Chi-square	138.829	0.0000	20	580
PP- Fisher Chi-square	146.098	0.0000	20	600

DROA				
Method	Statistic	Probability	Cross- sections	Observations
Null: Unit Root (assumes common unit root process)				

Levin, Lin & Chu	-21.6882	0.0000	20	578
Null: Unit Root (assumes individual unit root process)				
Im, Pesaran & Shin W- Stat	-22.5394	0.0000	20	578
ADF- Fisher Chi-square	419.813	0.0000	20	578
PP- Fisher Chi-square	541.853	0.0000	20	598

DSalesAssets				
Method	Statistic	Probability	Cross- sections	Observations
Null: Unit Root (assumes common unit root process)				
Levin, Lin & Chu	-22.7673	0.0000	20	578
Null: Unit Root (assumes individual unit root process)				
Im, Pesaran & Shin W- Stat	-23.3832	0.0000	20	578
ADF- Fisher Chi-square	450.078	0.0000	20	578
PP- Fisher Chi-square	456.254	0.0000	20	598

DSalesCurrent				
Method	Statistic	Probability	Cross- sections	Observations
Null: Unit Root (assumes common unit root process)				
Levin, Lin & Chu	-21.0953	0.0000	19	549
Null: Unit Root (assumes individual unit root process)				
Im, Pesaran & Shin W- Stat	-22.9712	0.0000	19	549
ADF- Fisher Chi-square	426.707	0.0000	19	549
PP- Fisher Chi-square	551.920	0.0000	19	568

Appendix VII. Vector Autoregression Estimates (VAR) with 8 lags

	DCDS	DCASH	DCURRENT	DEBIT	DLEV	DLNSIZE	DRISKFREE	DROA	DSALESASSETS	DSALESCURRENT	INIWO
DCDS(-1)	1.035967	-0.010832	0.059434	-1.902666	-0.001513	-0.000428	-0.001742	0.000752	-0.003751	0.020927	0.002019
	(0.05751)	(0.04776)	(0.06162)	(1.38415)	(0.00105)	(0.00077)	(0.00088)	(0.00042)	(0.00285)	(0.01908)	(0.00312)
	[18.0125]	[-0.22682]	[0.96450]	[-1.37461]	[-1.43502]	[-0.55900]	[-1.98368]	[1.80402]	[-1.31683]	[1.09667]	[0.64678]
DCDS(-2)	-0.550795	0.019186	-0.037558	1.501082	0.001371	-0.000343	-0.006821	-0.000507	0.005980	-0.007470	0.001536
	(0.04841)	(0.04019)	(0.05186)	(1.16496)	(0.00089)	(0.00064)	(0.00074)	(0.00035)	(0.00240)	(0.01606)	(0.00263)
	[-11.3787]	[0.47733]	[-0.72418]	[1.28853]	[1.54586]	[-0.53248]	[-9.22835]	[-1.44523]	[2.49462]	[-0.46509]	[0.58481]
DCDS(-3)	0.110116	0.004483	0.017120	-0.702504	-0.000238	-5.13E-06	0.003462	0.000588	0.004064	0.022943	5.56E-05
	(0.03892)	(0.03232)	(0.04170)	(0.93659)	(0.00071)	(0.00052)	(0.00059)	(0.00028)	(0.00193)	(0.01291)	(0.00211)
	[2.82954]	[0.13873]	[0.41059]	[-0.75007]	[-0.33377]	[-0.00991]	[5.82520]	[2.08636]	[2.10856]	[1.77688]	[0.02635]
DCDS(-4)	-0.660672	-0.008120	0.051369	0.377835	0.000373	0.000281	-0.003691	-0.000487	-0.001695	-0.004013	0.000232
	(0.02771)	(0.02301)	(0.02969)	(0.66692)	(0.00051)	(0.00037)	(0.00042)	(0.00020)	(0.00137)	(0.00919)	(0.00150)
	[-23.8409]	[-0.35290]	[1.73012]	[0.56654]	[0.73342]	[0.76168]	[-8.72331]	[-2.42375]	[-1.23518]	[-0.43649]	[0.15446]
DCDS(-5)	0.341056	0.004757	0.012747	-1.247683	-0.001171	-0.000918	-0.001173	0.000767	0.003896	0.032052	-5.97E-05
	(0.04851)	(0.04028)	(0.05197)	(1.16743)	(0.00089)	(0.00065)	(0.00074)	(0.00035)	(0.00240)	(0.01609)	(0.00263)
	[7.03081]	[0.11811]	[0.24525]	[-1.06874]	[-1.31691]	[-1.42157]	[-1.58374]	[2.18180]	[1.62172]	[1.99145]	[-0.02267]
DCDS(-6)	-0.060360	0.012602	0.013385	0.133533	0.000118	-0.000388	-0.005141	-9.11E-05	0.000668	0.000870	0.003118
	(0.02466)	(0.02048)	(0.02642)	(0.59348)	(0.00045)	(0.00033)	(0.00038)	(0.00018)	(0.00122)	(0.00818)	(0.00134)
	[-2.44768]	[0.61544]	[0.50659]	[0.22500]	[0.26100]	[-1.18194]	[-13.6516]	[-0.51013]	[0.54689]	[0.10636]	[2.33004]
DCDS(-7)	-0.175035	0.021594	0.036473	0.243265	-0.000424	-0.000101	-0.003826	0.000293	0.008374	0.009931	0.002560
	(0.02912)	(0.02418)	(0.03120)	(0.70075)	(0.00053)	(0.00039)	(0.00044)	(0.00021)	(0.00144)	(0.00966)	(0.00158)
	[-6.01133]	[0.89311]	[1.16911]	[0.34715]	[-0.79542]	[-0.26103]	[-8.60525]	[1.39119]	[5.80677]	[1.02795]	[1.62009]
DCDS(-8)	0.250899	0.016042	0.075120	-1.102764	-0.000892	-0.000238	-0.001516	3.04E-05	-0.000251	0.021017	0.000354
	(0.03056)	(0.02538)	(0.03275)	(0.73554)	(0.00056)	(0.00041)	(0.00047)	(0.00022)	(0.00151)	(0.01014)	(0.00166)
	[8.20921]	[0.63210]	[2.29403]	[-1.49925]	[-1.59186]	[-0.58530]	[-3.24717]	[0.13732]	[-0.16580]	[2.07257]	[0.21339]
DCASH(-1)	0.294831	-0.176248	0.097625	0.364805	0.000852	0.000265	-0.001435	0.000747	-0.004411	-0.014805	-0.011239
	(0.10914)	(0.09063)	(0.11693)	(2.62658)	(0.00200)	(0.00145)	(0.00167)	(0.00079)	(0.00541)	(0.03621)	(0.00592)
	[2.70143]	[-1.94479]	[0.83488]	[0.13889]	[0.42588]	[0.18274]	[-0.86123]	[0.94517]	[-0.81602]	[-0.40886]	[-1.89762]
DCASH(-2)	0.009454	-0.371195	-0.133886	0.132686	-0.000654	0.000404	0.001521	-0.000559	-0.001370	-0.002950	-0.014411
	(0.10604)	(0.08806)	(0.11362)	(2.55210)	(0.00194)	(0.00141)	(0.00162)	(0.00077)	(0.00525)	(0.03518)	(0.00575)
	[0.08915]	[-4.21544]	[-1.17839]	[0.05199]	[-0.33626]	[0.28595]	[0.93948]	[-0.72800]	[-0.26086]	[-0.08386]	[-2.50408]
DCASH(-3)	-0.102358	-0.046070	-0.185668	-1.037512	-0.000174	-0.001102	-0.003360	-0.000900	0.004693	0.010117	-0.001291
	(0.10489)	(0.08710)	(0.11239)	(2.52443)	(0.00192)	(0.00140)	(0.00160)	(0.00076)	(0.00519)	(0.03480)	(0.00569)
	[-0.97582]	[-0.52892]	[-1.65206]	[-0.41099]	[-0.09026]	[-0.78894]	[-2.09780]	[-1.18460]	[0.90339]	[0.29071]	[-0.22675]
DCASH(-4)	-0.159410	0.065511	0.230233	-1.148474	-0.002335	-0.002733	0.000856	-0.001963	-0.007745	-0.013030	-0.004415
	(0.10341)	(0.08587)	(0.11079)	(2.48867)	(0.00190)	(0.00138)	(0.00158)	(0.00075)	(0.00512)	(0.03431)	(0.00561)
	[-1.54156]	[0.76293]	[2.07802]	[-0.46148]	[-1.23214]	[-1.98532]	[0.54179]	[-2.62034]	[-1.51229]	[-0.37978]	[-0.78664]
DCASH(-5)	0.093345	0.559600	0.612276	-1.718936	1.07E-05	-0.002383	-0.002223	-0.000468	-0.000945	0.009983	0.012747
	(0.10596)	(0.08799)	(0.11353)	(2.55013)	(0.00194)	(0.00141)	(0.00162)	(0.00077)	(0.00525)	(0.03516)	(0.00575)
	[0.88093]	[6.35997]	[5.39308]	[-0.67406]	[0.00552]	[-1.68969]	[-1.37373]	[-0.61005]	[-0.18001]	[0.28396]	[2.21664]
DCASH(-6)	0.066556	-0.356902	-0.096450	-1.228450	-0.000846	-0.000833	-0.001381	-0.000171	-0.004879	0.017438	0.005533
	(0.11225)	(0.09321)	(0.12026)	(2.70137)	(0.00206)	(0.00149)	(0.00171)	(0.00081)	(0.00556)	(0.03724)	(0.00609)
	[0.59294]	[-3.82916]	[-0.80199]	[-0.45475]	[-0.41121]	[-0.55730]	[-0.80572]	[-0.21060]	[-0.87772]	[0.46822]	[0.90825]
DCASH(-7)	0.107042	-0.461115	-0.342035	0.363504	-0.000950	-0.000902	-0.000226	-0.000202	-0.017851	-0.021071	-0.015268
	(0.11698)	(0.09714)	(0.12533)	(2.81524)	(0.00214)	(0.00156)	(0.00179)	(0.00085)	(0.00579)	(0.03881)	(0.00635)
	[0.91506]	[-4.74716]	[-2.72903]	[0.12912]	[-0.44315]	[-0.57939]	[-0.12637]	[-0.23805]	[-3.08126]	[-0.54290]	[-2.40511]
DCASH(-8)	0.129801	-0.045772	0.233113	0.448563	-0.000303	0.000909	0.000327	-0.001287	-0.001237	-0.004509	-0.003639
	(0.11390)	(0.09458)	(0.12203)	(2.74112)	(0.00209)	(0.00152)	(0.00174)	(0.00083)	(0.00564)	(0.03779)	(0.00618)
	[1.13963]	[-0.48397]	[1.91025]	[0.16364]	[-0.14537]	[0.59940]	[0.18808]	[-1.55966]	[-0.21920]	[-0.11933]	[-0.58880]
DCURRENT(-1)	-0.297362	-0.465672	-0.811988	0.551638	-0.000618	0.000189	0.001142	-0.000774	0.005189	-0.004441	0.011466
	(0.08024)	(0.06662)	(0.08597)	(1.93097)	(0.00147)	(0.00107)	(0.00123)	(0.00058)	(0.00397)	(0.02662)	(0.00435)
	[-3.70613]	[-6.98945]	[-9.44550]	[0.28568]	[-0.41995]	[0.17680]	[0.93171]	[-1.33262]	[1.30572]	[-0.16681]	[2.63337]

DCURRENT(-2)	0.013909	0.025506	-0.252895	-0.160078	0.000838	1.91E-05	-0.001916	-0.000383	0.001785	-0.002022	0.017549
	(0.09250)	(0.07681)	(0.09911)	(2.22621)	(0.00170)	(0.00123)	(0.00141)	(0.00067)	(0.00458)	(0.03069)	(0.00502)
	[0.15036]	[0.33205]	[-2.55168]	[-0.07191]	[0.49401]	[0.01551]	[-1.35609]	[-0.57130]	[0.38963]	[-0.06587]	[3.49586]
DCURRENT(-3)	0.101996	-0.090822	-0.159929	0.807597	0.000451	0.000306	0.002971	-0.000316	-0.004371	-0.015631	0.002346
	(0.09200)	(0.07640)	(0.09857)	(2.21415)	(0.00169)	(0.00122)	(0.00140)	(0.00067)	(0.00456)	(0.03053)	(0.00499)
	[1.10864]	[-1.18885]	[-1.62245]	[0.36474]	[0.26771]	[0.24961]	[2.11476]	[-0.47396]	[-0.95934]	[-0.51209]	[0.46985]
DCURRENT(-4)	0.130500	-0.303532	-0.632806	1.220279	0.001365	0.000525	-0.000863	0.000290	0.002378	-0.015086	0.000139
	(0.09174)	(0.07618)	(0.09830)	(2.20794)	(0.00168)	(0.00122)	(0.00140)	(0.00066)	(0.00454)	(0.03044)	(0.00498)
	[1.42245]	[-3.98435]	[-6.43778]	[0.55268]	[0.81183]	[0.42954]	[-0.61581]	[0.43602]	[0.52341]	[-0.49560]	[0.02792]
DCURRENT(-5)	-0.092859	-0.730934	-0.951389	2.213431	-0.001002	0.000633	-8.55E-05	-0.000638	-0.000936	-0.029915	-0.018151
	(0.09253)	(0.07683)	(0.09914)	(2.22685)	(0.00170)	(0.00123)	(0.00141)	(0.00067)	(0.00458)	(0.03070)	(0.00502)
	[-1.00357]	[-9.51322]	[-9.59665]	[0.99398]	[-0.59083]	[0.51373]	[-0.06052]	[-0.95194]	[-0.20419]	[-0.97441]	[-3.61477]
DCURRENT(-6)	-0.012867	0.285263	-0.048817	0.668267	-0.000303	-0.000983	-0.000393	-0.001156	0.004324	-0.020764	-0.007811
	(0.10865)	(0.09022)	(0.11641)	(2.61480)	(0.00199)	(0.00145)	(0.00166)	(0.00079)	(0.00538)	(0.03605)	(0.00590)
	[-0.11842]	[3.16189]	[-0.41936]	[0.25557]	[-0.15229]	[-0.67974]	[-0.23683]	[-1.46920]	[0.80363]	[-0.57601]	[-1.32474]
DCURRENT(-7)	-0.064027	0.252832	0.013901	-1.261462	-0.000266	-0.000712	-0.000565	-0.001226	0.014627	0.017008	0.013235
	(0.10621)	(0.08819)	(0.11379)	(2.55601)	(0.00195)	(0.00141)	(0.00162)	(0.00077)	(0.00526)	(0.03524)	(0.00576)
	[-0.60285]	[2.86687]	[0.12216]	[-0.49353]	[-0.13651]	[-0.50333]	[-0.34823]	[-1.59356]	[2.78086]	[0.48266]	[2.29618]
DCURRENT(-8)	-0.096702	0.018768	-0.350374	-0.772498	-0.000585	-0.001893	-0.001559	-9.74E-05	0.000360	-0.005469	0.002772
	(0.10479)	(0.08702)	(0.11228)	(2.52200)	(0.00192)	(0.00139)	(0.00160)	(0.00076)	(0.00519)	(0.03477)	(0.00569)
	[-0.92279]	[0.21568]	[-3.12060]	[-0.30630]	[-0.30437]	[-1.35713]	[-0.97421]	[-0.12835]	[0.06934]	[-0.15730]	[0.48736]
DEBIT(-1)	-0.001672	0.000300	0.000433	-0.447937	9.81E-06	6.82E-05	6.36E-05	3.25E-05	-0.000123	6.72E-05	-0.000140
	(0.00227)	(0.00188)	(0.00243)	(0.05461)	(4.2E-05)	(3.0E-05)	(3.5E-05)	(1.6E-05)	(0.00011)	(0.00075)	(0.00012)
	[-0.73689]	[0.15916]	[0.17800]	[-8.20280]	[0.23599]	[2.25666]	[1.83691]	[1.97753]	[-1.09463]	[0.08922]	[-1.13737]
DEBIT(-2)	-0.001897	0.000648	0.001354	-0.538379	1.33E-05	3.44E-05	-3.31E-06	1.42E-05	-0.000210	-0.001381	-0.000110
	(0.00251)	(0.00208)	(0.00269)	(0.06032)	(4.6E-05)	(3.3E-05)	(3.8E-05)	(1.8E-05)	(0.00012)	(0.00083)	(0.00014)
	[-0.75696]	[0.31118]	[0.50408]	[-8.92584]	[0.29042]	[1.03136]	[-0.08639]	[0.78432]	[-1.68805]	[-1.66089]	[-0.81082]
DEBIT(-3)	-0.002594	-0.000780	-0.000559	-0.504429	1.70E-05	4.35E-05	3.04E-05	1.98E-05	-0.000113	-0.000966	-7.11E-05
	(0.00287)	(0.00239)	(0.00308)	(0.06915)	(5.3E-05)	(3.8E-05)	(4.4E-05)	(2.1E-05)	(0.00014)	(0.00095)	(0.00016)
	[-0.90271]	[-0.32713]	[-0.18145]	[-7.29507]	[0.32234]	[1.13670]	[0.69235]	[0.94930]	[-0.79340]	[-1.01318]	[-0.45585]
DEBIT(-4)	-0.000842	0.000166	-0.000417	-0.349671	-3.59E-05	4.83E-05	7.84E-05	7.19E-05	-0.000101	0.000955	-3.27E-05
	(0.00301)	(0.00250)	(0.00322)	(0.07233)	(5.5E-05)	(4.0E-05)	(4.6E-05)	(2.2E-05)	(0.00015)	(0.00100)	(0.00016)
	[-0.28018]	[0.06665]	[-0.12954]	[-4.83417]	[-0.65095]	[1.20712]	[1.70907]	[3.30073]	[-0.67900]	[0.95757]	[-0.20027]
DEBIT(-5)	-0.001375	0.000101	0.000236	-0.369374	2.81E-05	8.84E-05	-6.33E-06	4.04E-05	-9.86E-05	0.000511	-6.68E-05
	(0.00310)	(0.00258)	(0.00332)	(0.07465)	(5.7E-05)	(4.1E-05)	(4.7E-05)	(2.2E-05)	(0.00015)	(0.00103)	(0.00017)
	[-0.44344]	[0.03933]	[0.07091]	[-4.94836]	[0.49473]	[2.14222]	[-0.13375]	[1.79722]	[-0.64185]	[0.49639]	[-0.39678]
DEBIT(-6)	-0.000466	0.000503	0.000289	-0.347908	1.67E-05	4.86E-05	2.92E-05	4.67E-05	-0.000132	0.002089	5.91E-05
	(0.00300)	(0.00249)	(0.00321)	(0.07212)	(5.5E-05)	(4.0E-05)	(4.6E-05)	(2.2E-05)	(0.00015)	(0.00099)	(0.00016)
	[-0.15564]	[0.20222]	[0.08988]	[-4.82420]	[0.30377]	[1.21932]	[0.63913]	[2.15245]	[-0.89176]	[2.10136]	[0.36363]
DEBIT(-7)	-0.005740	0.000291	-0.000181	-0.276562	3.67E-05	5.48E-05	8.40E-05	6.26E-05	-0.000130	0.002358	-3.13E-05
	(0.00286)	(0.00237)	(0.00306)	(0.06879)	(5.2E-05)	(3.8E-05)	(4.4E-05)	(2.1E-05)	(0.00014)	(0.00095)	(0.00016)
	[-2.00835]	[0.12247]	[-0.05898]	[-4.02051]	[0.69994]	[1.44070]	[1.92538]	[3.02221]	[-0.92143]	[2.48627]	[-0.20196]
DEBIT(-8)	0.003038	0.000738	0.001073	0.097369	0.000106	6.07E-05	-1.10E-05	-1.11E-05	-0.000354	0.000138	-1.57E-05
	(0.00283)	(0.00235)	(0.00303)	(0.06810)	(5.2E-05)	(3.8E-05)	(4.3E-05)	(2.0E-05)	(0.00014)	(0.00094)	(0.00015)
	[1.07350]	[0.31419]	[0.35405]	[1.42982]	[2.04582]	[1.61245]	[-0.25431]	[-0.54258]	[-2.52621]	[0.14664]	[-0.10228]
DLEV(-1)	1.860058	-2.529018	-1.708769	-68.06497	-0.458031	-0.087060	0.040131	-0.028412	0.127978	-2.861454	0.025218
	(6.15336)	(5.10957)	(6.59283)	(148.089)	(0.11278)	(0.08191)	(0.09397)	(0.04457)	(0.30475)	(2.04162)	(0.33394)
	[0.30228]	[-0.49496]	[-0.25919]	[-0.45962]	[-4.06127]	[-1.06291]	[0.42708]	[-0.63746]	[0.41994]	[-1.40156]	[0.07552]
DLEV(-2)	8.050103	-1.215817	3.660045	-204.6699	-0.158192	-0.066944	0.004800	-0.085347	0.489063	-4.452924	0.842969
	(6.70676)	(5.56910)	(7.18576)	(161.408)	(0.12292)	(0.08927)	(0.10242)	(0.04858)	(0.33216)	(2.22523)	(0.36397)
	[1.20030]	[-0.21831]	[0.50935]	[-1.26803]	[-1.28692]	[-0.74987]	[0.04687]	[-1.75684]	[1.47238]	[-2.00110]	[2.31604]
DLEV(-3)	2.843719	7.920699	4.914389	-356.6390	-0.083114	-0.148440	0.031990	-0.022254	0.108602	4.486766	0.261959

	(6.99912)	(5.81187)	(7.49900)	(168.444)	(0.12828)	(0.09317)	(0.10688)	(0.05070)	(0.34664)	(2.32224)	(0.37984)
	[0.40630]	[1.36285]	[0.65534]	[-2.11726]	[-0.64791]	[-1.59329]	[0.29931]	[-0.43896]	[0.31330]	[1.93209]	[0.68966]
DLEV(-4)	-7.065988	-9.712473	-5.970890	54.32112	0.152734	0.060189	0.006193	0.002080	0.324143	0.528085	-0.632342
	(6.87127)	(5.70571)	(7.36203)	(165.367)	(0.12594)	(0.09146)	(0.10493)	(0.04977)	(0.34031)	(2.27982)	(0.37290)
	[-1.02834]	[-1.70224]	[-0.81104]	[0.32849]	[1.21276]	[0.65807]	[0.05902]	[0.04179]	[0.95250]	[0.23163]	[-1.69575]
DLEV(-5)	7.536375	-6.693372	-1.620983	18.47783	-0.014826	-0.163009	-0.111462	-0.011314	0.727616	0.515902	-0.571874
	(6.97156)	(5.78898)	(7.46948)	(167.781)	(0.12778)	(0.09280)	(0.10646)	(0.05050)	(0.34527)	(2.31309)	(0.37834)
	[1.08102]	[-1.15623]	[-0.21701]	[0.11013]	[-0.11603]	[-1.75659]	[-1.04699]	[-0.22405]	[2.10737]	[0.22304]	[-1.51153]
DLEV(-6)	-2.689732	1.711207	5.091677	-35.35849	-0.058200	-0.059155	0.085705	0.028119	0.091065	1.496738	-0.565304
	(6.74604)	(5.60172)	(7.22785)	(162.353)	(0.12364)	(0.08980)	(0.10302)	(0.04886)	(0.33410)	(2.23827)	(0.36610)
	[-0.39871]	[0.30548]	[0.70445]	[-0.21779]	[-0.47071]	[-0.65876]	[0.83196]	[0.57545]	[0.27257]	[0.66870]	[-1.54412]
DLEV(-7)	1.769835	4.964190	0.575258	-179.5716	0.053681	0.042212	-0.178874	-0.027851	-0.417238	-5.490132	0.392953
	(5.59330)	(4.64451)	(5.99278)	(134.611)	(0.10252)	(0.07445)	(0.08541)	(0.04051)	(0.27701)	(1.85580)	(0.30354)
	[0.31642]	[1.06883]	[0.09599]	[-1.33401]	[0.52364]	[0.56697]	[-2.09422]	[-0.68744]	[-1.50620]	[-2.95837]	[1.29455]
DLEV(-8)	-9.391035	0.630304	0.104026	-169.6195	0.037734	-0.012709	-0.000972	-0.079782	-0.051219	-2.407484	0.727303
	(4.63544)	(3.84914)	(4.96651)	(111.559)	(0.08496)	(0.06170)	(0.07079)	(0.03358)	(0.22957)	(1.53799)	(0.25156)
	[-2.02592]	[0.16375]	[0.02095]	[-1.52045]	[0.44414]	[-0.20597]	[-0.01374]	[-2.37612]	[-0.22311]	[-1.56534]	[2.89116]
DLNSIZE(-1)	-8.782151	-1.778223	-4.091374	86.20305	0.222438	-0.070972	-0.014717	-0.038808	-0.167934	0.100322	-0.007795
	(5.32934)	(4.42533)	(5.70997)	(128.258)	(0.09768)	(0.07094)	(0.08138)	(0.03860)	(0.26394)	(1.76822)	(0.28922)
	[-1.64789]	[-0.40183]	[-0.71653]	[0.67211]	[2.27727]	[-1.00046]	[-0.18084]	[-1.00532]	[-0.63626]	[0.05674]	[-0.02695]
DLNSIZE(-2)	0.109011	7.633027	9.046038	72.84724	0.010455	-0.042293	-0.137928	-0.035083	-0.429023	0.868936	-0.471725
	(5.42372)	(4.50370)	(5.81109)	(130.530)	(0.09941)	(0.07220)	(0.08282)	(0.03929)	(0.26861)	(1.79953)	(0.29434)
	[0.02010]	[1.69483]	[1.55669]	[0.55809]	[0.10517]	[-0.58582]	[-1.66532]	[-0.89300]	[-1.59717]	[0.48287]	[-1.60265]
DLNSIZE(-3)	-2.688918	1.346501	3.136984	202.1612	0.067181	0.127274	0.093165	0.022276	-0.011918	-2.723076	-0.145687
	(5.39580)	(4.48051)	(5.78117)	(129.858)	(0.09890)	(0.07182)	(0.08240)	(0.03908)	(0.26723)	(1.79027)	(0.29283)
	[-0.49834]	[0.30052]	[0.54262]	[1.55679]	[0.67931]	[1.77203]	[1.13068]	[0.56995]	[-0.04460]	[-1.52104]	[-0.49752]
DLNSIZE(-4)	7.038916	2.196557	-0.104313	-62.20374	-0.053176	0.069742	0.043200	-0.013681	0.053916	0.144890	0.226324
	(3.25156)	(2.70000)	(3.48379)	(78.2534)	(0.05960)	(0.04328)	(0.04965)	(0.02355)	(0.16104)	(1.07883)	(0.17646)
	[2.16478]	[0.81354]	[-0.02994]	[-0.79490]	[-0.89229]	[1.61136]	[0.87003]	[-0.58088]	[0.33481]	[0.13430]	[1.28259]
DLNSIZE(-5)	0.892487	2.139289	-0.607794	-52.99411	0.018495	0.109874	0.073578	-0.008836	-0.231209	-0.771390	0.119541
	(2.93467)	(2.43687)	(3.14427)	(70.6271)	(0.05379)	(0.03906)	(0.04481)	(0.02126)	(0.14534)	(0.97369)	(0.15926)
	[0.30412]	[0.87788]	[-0.19330]	[-0.75034]	[0.34386]	[2.81270]	[1.64185]	[-0.41568]	[-1.59079]	[-0.79223]	[0.75060]
DLNSIZE(-6)	2.711971	0.273434	-1.720556	-11.49013	0.037889	0.083973	-0.042592	-0.011818	0.154332	-1.110848	0.124338
	(2.46937)	(2.05049)	(2.64573)	(59.4288)	(0.04526)	(0.03287)	(0.03771)	(0.01789)	(0.12230)	(0.81931)	(0.13401)
	[1.09825]	[0.13335]	[-0.65031]	[-0.19334]	[0.83715]	[2.55472]	[-1.12950]	[-0.66069]	[1.26194]	[-1.35583]	[0.92782]
DLNSIZE(-7)	2.093876	0.926699	1.275624	34.47380	-0.002314	0.033835	0.039604	0.020384	0.174532	0.515974	-0.078754
	(1.44506)	(1.19994)	(1.54827)	(34.7775)	(0.02649)	(0.01924)	(0.02207)	(0.01047)	(0.07157)	(0.47946)	(0.07842)
	[1.44899]	[0.77229]	[0.82390]	[0.99127]	[-0.08738]	[1.75901]	[1.79473]	[1.94741]	[2.43869]	[1.07616]	[-1.00423]
DLNSIZE(-8)	0.517313	0.641320	0.306350	24.23059	0.007982	0.040768	0.030603	0.011956	0.119499	0.401071	-0.122267
	(1.01761)	(0.84500)	(1.09029)	(24.4903)	(0.01865)	(0.01355)	(0.01554)	(0.00737)	(0.05040)	(0.33763)	(0.05522)
	[0.50836]	[0.75896]	[0.28098]	[0.98939]	[0.42795]	[3.00973]	[1.96933]	[1.62197]	[2.37111]	[1.18789]	[-2.21399]
DRISKFREE(-1)	25.01876	0.305098	1.110995	-60.47824	-0.066293	-0.043534	0.092259	0.083226	0.033039	1.461803	-0.060265
	(3.45403)	(2.86813)	(3.70072)	(83.1262)	(0.06331)	(0.04598)	(0.05275)	(0.02502)	(0.17106)	(1.14601)	(0.18745)
	[7.24335]	[0.10638]	[0.30021]	[-0.72755]	[-1.04717]	[-0.94688]	[1.74914]	[3.32650]	[0.19314]	[1.27556]	[-0.32150]
DRISKFREE(-2)	-2.341319	1.216132	2.916819	38.23365	0.064385	0.004130	0.088116	0.013235	0.134610	-0.615354	-0.017559
	(2.67499)	(2.22123)	(2.86604)	(64.3774)	(0.04903)	(0.03561)	(0.04085)	(0.01938)	(0.13248)	(0.88753)	(0.14517)
	[-0.87526]	[0.54750]	[1.01772]	[0.59390]	[1.31324]	[0.11600]	[2.15712]	[0.68305]	[1.01607]	[-0.69333]	[-0.12095]
DRISKFREE(-3)	-106.0460	-2.030237	-3.340264	141.6999	-0.024213	0.010105	-0.491894	-0.038883	0.248300	-0.058965	0.023517
	(2.49843)	(2.07463)	(2.67687)	(60.1283)	(0.04579)	(0.03326)	(0.03815)	(0.01810)	(0.12374)	(0.82895)	(0.13559)

		[-42.4450]	[-0.97860]	[-1.24782)	[2.35663)	[-0.52876]	[0.30385)	[-12.8928)	[-2.14859)	[2.00667)	[-0.07113)	[0.17345)
DRISKFRE E(-4)	195.5826	-1.939125	2.074489	-246.1490	-0.245454	-0.084124	-0.246885	0.097406	-0.556492	3.225544	0.220678
	(7.17811)	(5.96050)	(7.69078)	(172.751)	(0.13156)	(0.09555)	(0.10961)	(0.05199)	(0.35550)	(2.38162)	(0.38955)
	[27.2471)	[-0.32533)	[0.26974)	[-1.42487)	[-1.86569)	[-0.88044)	[-2.25231)	[1.87340)	[-1.56537)	[1.35435)	[0.56650)
DRISKFRE E(-5)	-102.5123	3.893601	-3.419817	286.8897	0.245979	0.015881	-0.713419	-0.075946	0.798032	-3.181282	-0.159442
	(8.77338)	(7.28516)	(9.39998)	(211.144)	(0.16080)	(0.11678)	(0.13397)	(0.06355)	(0.43451)	(2.91091)	(0.47612)
	[-11.6845)	[0.53446)	[-0.36381)	[1.35874)	[1.52971)	[0.13599)	[-5.32502)	[-1.19506)	[1.83663)	[-1.09288)	[-0.33488)
DRISKFRE E(-6)	-12.27554	1.701010	3.313706	-130.1602	-0.083935	-0.020090	0.700194	0.065049	0.188569	3.003297	-0.152025
	(5.42447)	(4.50432)	(5.81189)	(130.548)	(0.09942)	(0.07221)	(0.08283)	(0.03929)	(0.26865)	(1.79978)	(0.29438)
	[-2.26299)	[0.37764)	[0.57016)	[-0.99703)	[-0.84424)	[-0.27823)	[8.45288)	[1.65553)	[0.70191)	[1.66870)	[-0.51642)
DRISKFRE E(-7)	22.47164	-4.266900	5.264163	-7.753645	-0.067205	0.037746	-0.374446	-0.017284	-1.040603	-1.664364	0.058618
	(3.87162)	(3.21488)	(4.14813)	(93.1759)	(0.07096)	(0.05154)	(0.05912)	(0.02804)	(0.19175)	(1.28456)	(0.21011)
	[5.80420)	[-1.32724)	[1.26904)	[-0.08322)	[-0.94708)	[0.73244)	[-6.33345)	[-0.61632)	[-5.42701)	[-1.29567)	[0.27899)
DRISKFRE E(-8)	12.98226	2.198254	-3.597769	39.84426	-0.019511	-0.083815	-0.467342	0.048260	0.682378	1.381828	-0.092809
	(3.64999)	(3.03085)	(3.91068)	(87.8422)	(0.06690)	(0.04859)	(0.05574)	(0.02644)	(0.18077)	(1.21103)	(0.19808)
	[3.55679)	[0.72529)	[-0.91999)	[0.45359)	[-0.29165)	[-1.72512)	[-8.38468)	[1.82538)	[3.77486)	[1.14104)	[-0.46854)
DROA(-1)	10.20356	2.177860	-0.196749	-203.1107	-0.237206	-0.028167	-0.182371	-0.496608	0.954816	2.982762	-0.992947
	(8.60109)	(7.14210)	(9.21539)	(206.997)	(0.15764)	(0.11449)	(0.13134)	(0.06230)	(0.42598)	(2.85375)	(0.46677)
	[1.18631)	[0.30493)	[-0.02135)	[-0.98122)	[-1.50470)	[-0.24602)	[-1.38850)	[-7.97105)	[2.24148)	[1.04521)	[-2.12726)
DROA(-2)	16.93096	-6.383791	-8.866406	-318.6899	-0.241994	-0.028398	-0.087534	-0.345798	0.716840	1.445594	-0.190097
	(9.77535)	(8.11717)	(10.4735)	(235.258)	(0.17917)	(0.13012)	(0.14928)	(0.07081)	(0.48413)	(3.24336)	(0.53050)
	[1.73201)	[-0.78646)	[-0.84655)	[-1.35464)	[-1.35067)	[-0.21825)	[-0.58639)	[-4.88366)	[1.48067)	[0.44571)	[-0.35834)
DROA(-3)	18.97283	3.637168	6.918402	-464.7579	-0.397038	-0.249545	-0.067760	-0.335362	0.723923	8.210273	-0.260365
	(10.2019)	(8.47137)	(10.9305)	(245.523)	(0.18698)	(0.13580)	(0.15579)	(0.07390)	(0.50526)	(3.38489)	(0.55365)
	[1.85973)	[0.42935)	[0.63294)	[-1.89293)	[-2.12339)	[-1.83762)	[-0.43495)	[-4.53824)	[1.43278)	[2.42557)	[-0.47027)
DROA(-4)	8.331232	-6.528494	-6.230284	-438.3511	-0.111323	0.022233	-0.106663	0.113924	0.476538	1.498277	0.036211
	(10.6482)	(8.84199)	(11.4087)	(256.265)	(0.19516)	(0.14174)	(0.16261)	(0.07713)	(0.52736)	(3.53297)	(0.57787)
	[0.78241)	[-0.73835)	[-0.54610)	[-1.71054)	[-0.57041)	[0.15686)	[-0.65596)	[1.47704)	[0.90362)	[0.42408)	[0.06266)
DROA(-5)	13.08706	4.808517	10.13657	-249.9697	-0.217230	-0.025672	-0.009921	-0.020483	0.496845	0.822550	0.119815
	(10.3962)	(8.63269)	(11.1387)	(250.199)	(0.19054)	(0.13838)	(0.15876)	(0.07530)	(0.51488)	(3.44934)	(0.56419)
	[1.25883)	[0.55701)	[0.91003)	[-0.99908)	[-1.14005)	[-0.18551)	[-0.06249)	[-0.27200)	[0.96497)	[0.23847)	[0.21237)
DROA(-6)	3.295638	13.52449	22.17965	-223.3704	-0.130527	-0.138673	0.105942	-0.160140	0.576668	1.430129	-0.149039
	(9.80448)	(8.14135)	(10.5047)	(235.959)	(0.17970)	(0.13051)	(0.14972)	(0.07102)	(0.48558)	(3.25302)	(0.53208)
	[0.33614)	[1.66121)	[2.11140)	[-0.94665)	[-0.72636)	[-1.06257)	[0.70760)	[-2.25491)	[1.18760)	[0.43963)	[-0.28011)
DROA(-7)	6.620528	14.09571	15.99786	-226.8925	0.024835	-0.076208	-0.050162	-0.189814	0.434337	-1.907651	-0.032891
	(9.04862)	(7.51371)	(9.69488)	(217.768)	(0.16585)	(0.12045)	(0.13818)	(0.06554)	(0.44814)	(3.00224)	(0.49106)
	[0.73166)	[1.87600)	[1.65014)	[-1.04190)	[0.14975)	[-0.63271)	[-0.36303)	[-2.89601)	[0.96920)	[-0.63541)	[-0.06698)
DROA(-8)	8.398835	6.288170	8.165370	-119.3695	-0.298268	-0.120744	0.029340	0.111579	0.227388	-0.335763	-0.942199
	(8.01259)	(6.65342)	(8.58485)	(192.834)	(0.14686)	(0.10666)	(0.12236)	(0.05804)	(0.39683)	(2.65849)	(0.43484)
	[1.04820)	[0.94510)	[0.95114)	[-0.61903)	[-2.03101)	[-1.13209)	[0.23979)	[1.92249)	[0.57301)	[-0.12630)	[-2.16679)
DSALESAS SETS(-1)	3.583401	-0.474487	-1.820606	-1.863690	0.005599	-0.001690	-0.051146	0.000787	-0.890625	-0.192356	-0.014653
	(1.27991)	(1.06280)	(1.37133)	(30.8029)	(0.02346)	(0.01704)	(0.01955)	(0.00927)	(0.06339)	(0.42466)	(0.06946)
	[2.79972)	[-0.44645)	[-1.32762)	[-0.06050)	[0.23869)	[-0.09922)	[-2.61682)	[0.08488)	[-14.0502)	[-0.45296)	[-0.21095)
DSALESAS SETS(-2)	-0.517491	0.682048	-0.421205	17.38895	0.006060	0.004205	0.016698	0.012582	-0.762377	-0.018184	0.000766
	(1.61728)	(1.34294)	(1.73279)	(38.9221)	(0.02964)	(0.02153)	(0.02470)	(0.01171)	(0.08010)	(0.53660)	(0.08777)
	[-0.31998)	[0.50788)	[-0.24308)	[0.44676)	[0.20443)	[0.19532)	[0.67613)	[1.07400)	[-9.51815)	[-0.03389)	[0.00872)
DSALESAS SETS(-3)	0.922713	-1.002118	-2.087405	8.038919	-0.000761	0.003060	-0.015336	0.003616	-0.762864	-0.155698	0.054510
	(1.89362)	(1.57241)	(2.02887)	(45.5727)	(0.03471)	(0.02521)	(0.02892)	(0.01372)	(0.09378)	(0.62828)	(0.10277)
	[0.48727)	[-0.63731)	[-1.02885)	[0.17640)	[-0.02194)	[0.12140)	[-0.53035)	[0.26365)	[-8.13433)	[-0.24782)	[0.53043)
DSALESAS SETS(-4)	0.644242	0.341047	-1.158505	19.88705	-0.009313	-0.006411	0.028481	-0.002134	-0.197401	1.050999	0.079899
	(2.10680)	(1.74943)	(2.25727)	(50.7032)	(0.03861)	(0.02804)	(0.03217)	(0.01526)	(0.10434)	(0.69902)	(0.11433)

	[0.30579]	[0.19495]	[-0.51323]	[0.39222]	[-0.24118]	[-0.22860]	[0.88527]	[-0.13981]	[-1.89188]	[1.50354]	[0.69882]
DSALESAS SETS(-5)	-4.831001	-0.663618	-2.055453	-25.35645	-0.002796	0.008253	0.098919	0.001938	-0.197402	1.030122	0.048121
	(2.01855)	(1.67615)	(2.16272)	(48.5793)	(0.03700)	(0.02687)	(0.03082)	(0.01462)	(0.09997)	(0.66973)	(0.10955)
	[-2.39330]	[-0.39592]	[-0.95040]	[-0.52196]	[-0.07557]	[0.30716]	[3.20910]	[0.13251]	[-1.97460]	[1.53810]	[0.43928]
DSALESAS SETS(-6)	5.103745	-2.924337	-4.583227	10.42982	0.016777	0.040881	-0.001197	-0.003099	-0.368653	0.227876	-0.090527
	(1.85212)	(1.53795)	(1.98440)	(44.5739)	(0.03395)	(0.02465)	(0.02828)	(0.01342)	(0.09173)	(0.61451)	(0.10051)
	[2.75562]	[-1.90145]	[-2.30963]	[0.23399]	[0.49422]	[1.65822]	[-0.04232]	[-0.23102]	[-4.01899]	[0.37082]	[-0.90065]
DSALESAS SETS(-7)	3.782241	-0.307639	-2.008907	24.71774	0.032893	0.022313	0.016156	0.005414	-0.207267	0.007334	-0.052363
	(1.65182)	(1.37163)	(1.76980)	(39.7535)	(0.03028)	(0.02199)	(0.02522)	(0.01196)	(0.08181)	(0.54806)	(0.08964)
	[2.28974]	[-0.22429]	[-1.13511]	[0.62178]	[1.08646]	[1.01482]	[0.64048]	[0.45251]	[-2.53358]	[0.01338]	[-0.58413]
DSALESAS SETS(-8)	-3.705919	0.148713	-1.926346	1.991519	0.039613	0.030232	0.022201	0.016044	0.124987	-0.035122	-0.029492
	(1.22563)	(1.01773)	(1.31316)	(29.4965)	(0.02246)	(0.01631)	(0.01872)	(0.00888)	(0.06070)	(0.40665)	(0.06651)
	[-3.02369]	[0.14612]	[-1.46695]	[0.06752]	[1.76341]	[1.85310]	[1.18619]	[1.80725]	[2.05908]	[-0.08637]	[-0.44340]
DSALESCU RRENT(-1)	0.149232	0.096855	0.151608	-2.971443	-0.001376	-0.001011	-0.002570	-0.000450	0.008019	-0.743200	0.010160
	(0.19660)	(0.16325)	(0.21064)	(4.73152)	(0.00360)	(0.00262)	(0.00300)	(0.00142)	(0.00974)	(0.06523)	(0.01067)
	[0.75906]	[0.59328]	[0.71973]	[-0.62801]	[-0.38177]	[-0.38624]	[-0.85588]	[-0.31574]	[0.82361]	[-11.3934]	[0.95222]
DSALESCU RRENT(-2)	0.128338	0.227981	0.286535	-7.582946	-0.002552	-0.002087	3.19E-05	0.000269	-0.005297	-0.690599	0.006182
	(0.23697)	(0.19677)	(0.25390)	(5.70303)	(0.00434)	(0.00315)	(0.00362)	(0.00172)	(0.01174)	(0.07862)	(0.01286)
	[0.54158]	[1.15859]	[1.12856]	[-1.32963]	[-0.58749]	[-0.66165]	[0.00883]	[0.15654]	[-0.45134]	[-8.78353]	[0.48069]
DSALESCU RRENT(-3)	0.152565	0.218270	0.268592	-8.073324	-0.000689	0.000739	-0.003149	0.001229	0.007213	-0.608082	-0.012014
	(0.26199)	(0.21755)	(0.28070)	(6.30508)	(0.00480)	(0.00349)	(0.00400)	(0.00190)	(0.01298)	(0.08692)	(0.01422)
	[0.58234]	[1.00333]	[0.95687]	[-1.28045]	[-0.14346]	[0.21199]	[-0.78722]	[0.64786]	[0.55593]	[-6.99552]	[-0.84503]
DSALESCU RRENT(-4)	-0.381450	-0.037966	0.066935	-9.590827	0.003053	0.002177	-0.000114	0.000900	0.023043	-0.271926	-0.018009
	(0.28053)	(0.23294)	(0.30056)	(6.75124)	(0.00514)	(0.00373)	(0.00428)	(0.00203)	(0.01389)	(0.09308)	(0.01522)
	[-1.35977]	[-0.16299]	[0.22270]	[-1.42060]	[0.59385]	[0.58306]	[-0.02665]	[0.44274]	[1.65857]	[-2.92157]	[-1.18294]
DSALESCU RRENT(-5)	0.065997	-0.077218	-0.055658	-4.549151	0.000593	0.001592	-0.002261	0.000807	0.010857	-0.237883	-0.029609
	(0.29438)	(0.24444)	(0.31540)	(7.08465)	(0.00540)	(0.00392)	(0.00450)	(0.00213)	(0.01458)	(0.09767)	(0.01598)
	[0.22419]	[-0.31589]	[-0.17646]	[-0.64211]	[0.10999]	[0.40639]	[-0.50307]	[0.37828]	[0.74469]	[-2.43554]	[-1.85336]
DSALESCU RRENT(-6)	-0.179685	0.105039	0.034599	-4.306031	0.003434	0.003316	-0.004277	-0.001186	0.001883	-0.229459	0.010652
	(0.29388)	(0.24403)	(0.31487)	(7.07259)	(0.00539)	(0.00391)	(0.00449)	(0.00213)	(0.01455)	(0.09751)	(0.01595)
	[-0.61143]	[0.43044]	[0.10988]	[-0.60883]	[0.63749]	[0.84758]	[-0.95308]	[-0.55734]	[0.12936]	[-2.35329]	[0.66792]
DSALESCU RRENT(-7)	-0.035863	0.130711	0.171491	-4.193901	0.001733	0.002571	-0.005294	-0.001666	-0.007982	-0.189941	0.007858
	(0.26984)	(0.22406)	(0.28911)	(6.49399)	(0.00495)	(0.00359)	(0.00412)	(0.00195)	(0.01336)	(0.08953)	(0.01464)
	[-0.13291]	[0.58336]	[0.59317]	[-0.64581]	[0.35034]	[0.71584]	[-1.28472]	[-0.85236]	[-0.59727]	[-2.12156]	[0.53659]
DSALESCU RRENT(-8)	-0.257465	0.080754	0.099554	0.522007	0.001238	0.001162	-0.002797	0.000158	-0.005409	0.019222	0.001658
	(0.25449)	(0.21132)	(0.27267)	(6.12470)	(0.00466)	(0.00339)	(0.00389)	(0.00184)	(0.01260)	(0.08444)	(0.01381)
	[-1.01168]	[0.38214]	[0.36511]	[0.08523]	[0.26534]	[0.34299]	[-0.71961]	[0.08596]	[-0.42913]	[0.22765]	[0.12002]
INIWO(-1)	0.230839	0.147814	-2.192335	-10.09078	0.002128	0.002645	-0.006944	-0.010362	0.008641	0.286968	0.520609
	(1.08669)	(0.90236)	(1.16430)	(26.1528)	(0.01992)	(0.01446)	(0.01659)	(0.00787)	(0.05382)	(0.36055)	(0.05897)
	[0.21242]	[0.16381]	[-1.88296]	[-0.38584]	[0.10682]	[0.18282]	[-0.41845]	[-1.31644]	[0.16056]	[0.79591]	[8.82781]
INIWO(-2)	-2.900587	1.309597	0.454484	-9.661344	-0.036114	-0.014730	-0.009709	0.002034	-0.123368	0.593783	0.039125
	(1.18039)	(0.98016)	(1.26470)	(28.4078)	(0.02163)	(0.01571)	(0.01803)	(0.00855)	(0.05846)	(0.39164)	(0.06406)
	[-2.45731]	[1.33610]	[0.35936]	[-0.34009]	[-1.66929]	[-0.93747]	[-0.53863]	[0.23794]	[-2.11030]	[1.51614]	[0.61077]
INIWO(-3)	-0.360407	-2.078938	-1.593318	-8.862365	0.020479	-0.028243	-0.010361	0.007624	0.147185	0.336228	2.32E-06
	(1.28717)	(1.06883)	(1.37911)	(30.9777)	(0.02359)	(0.01713)	(0.01966)	(0.00932)	(0.06375)	(0.42707)	(0.06985)
	[-0.28000]	[-1.94506]	[-1.15533]	[-0.28609]	[0.86804]	[-1.64842]	[-0.52713]	[0.81766]	[2.30885]	[0.78729]	[3.3e-05]
INIWO(-4)	0.464658	-0.727798	-0.403716	-5.778334	0.004733	0.014757	0.035682	0.006310	0.052376	-0.345713	0.512082
	(1.29667)	(1.07671)	(1.38928)	(31.2061)	(0.02377)	(0.01726)	(0.01980)	(0.00939)	(0.06422)	(0.43022)	(0.07037)
	[0.35835]	[-0.67594]	[-0.29059]	[-0.18517]	[0.19915]	[0.85499]	[1.80203]	[0.67182]	[0.81558]	[-0.80357]	[7.27710]

INIWO(-5)	-1.278996	2.205944	2.991132	28.73542	-0.021582	-0.005844	-0.017992	0.012605	-0.013663	-0.344645	-0.199005
	(1.28496)	(1.06699)	(1.37673)	(30.9244)	(0.02355)	(0.01710)	(0.01962)	(0.00931)	(0.06364)	(0.42634)	(0.06973)
	[-0.99536]	[2.06744]	[2.17263]	[0.92922]	[-0.91641]	[-0.34169]	[-0.91693]	[1.35429]	[-0.21469]	[-0.80839]	[-2.85380]
INIWO(-6)	1.045918	-0.625863	-0.256050	12.37031	0.021929	0.026894	0.020540	-0.003781	0.097955	1.200517	-0.001128
	(1.23532)	(1.02577)	(1.32354)	(29.7296)	(0.02264)	(0.01644)	(0.01886)	(0.00895)	(0.06118)	(0.40986)	(0.06704)
	[0.84668]	[-0.61014]	[-0.19346]	[0.41609]	[0.96853]	[1.63554]	[1.08884]	[-0.42252]	[1.60109]	[2.92906]	[-0.01683]
INIWO(-7)	-0.668395	1.674365	2.240237	-14.00717	0.007222	0.001216	0.025162	-0.000538	-0.089099	-1.705860	-0.118800
	(1.26319)	(1.04892)	(1.35341)	(30.4004)	(0.02315)	(0.01681)	(0.01929)	(0.00915)	(0.06256)	(0.41911)	(0.06855)
	[-0.52913]	[1.59628]	[1.65526]	[-0.46076]	[0.31195]	[0.07234]	[1.30442]	[-0.05877]	[-1.42421]	[-4.07017]	[-1.73298]
INIWO(-8)	0.014577	-1.662524	-2.877030	35.86756	0.007907	0.005713	-0.037002	0.010078	0.054560	0.254949	0.105623
	(1.30076)	(1.08011)	(1.39366)	(31.3047)	(0.02384)	(0.01731)	(0.01986)	(0.00942)	(0.06442)	(0.43158)	(0.07059)
	[0.01121]	[-1.53921]	[-2.06437]	[1.14576]	[0.33164]	[0.32993]	[-1.86283]	[1.06963]	[0.84692]	[0.59073]	[1.49627]
C	3.787615	-0.343905	-0.353871	8.267940	-0.008887	-0.004385	-0.103437	0.004931	-0.011497	0.058148	-0.005744
	(0.43849)	(0.36411)	(0.46981)	(10.5529)	(0.00804)	(0.00584)	(0.00670)	(0.00318)	(0.02172)	(0.14549)	(0.02380)
	[8.63786]	[-0.94451]	[-0.75323]	[0.78348]	[-1.10580]	[-0.75131]	[-15.4475]	[1.55250]	[-0.52941]	[0.39968]	[-0.24138]
R-squared	0.956303	0.728680	0.696030	0.426986	0.229322	0.301951	0.911097	0.686175	0.835361	0.738964	0.636572
Adj. R-squared	0.942569	0.643408	0.600496	0.246896	-0.012892	0.082564	0.883156	0.587545	0.783618	0.656924	0.522351
Sum sq. resids	3708.008	2556.732	4256.580	2147651.	1.245614	0.656996	0.864677	0.194550	9.095050	408.1936	10.92058
S.E. equation	3.639078	3.021785	3.898983	87.57957	0.066698	0.048440	0.055571	0.026359	0.180229	1.207408	0.197489
F-statistic	69.63290	8.545360	7.285720	2.370956	0.946776	1.376338	32.60797	6.957018	16.14426	9.007381	5.573188
Log likelihood	-949.3135	-880.7228	-974.7692	-2123.035	526.4322	644.4578	593.7799	868.9927	159.6274	-542.2126	125.8789
Akaike AIC	5.627715	5.255950	5.765687	11.98935	-2.370906	-3.010612	-2.735935	-4.227603	-0.382804	3.421207	-0.199886
Schwarz SC	6.570970	6.199205	6.708941	12.93260	-1.427652	-2.067357	-1.792680	-3.284348	0.560450	4.364461	0.743369
Mean dependent	3.838370	-0.063455	-0.109582	-1.010339	0.000967	0.006300	-0.065060	0.001472	0.017862	0.078945	0.089431
S.D. dependent	15.18512	5.060317	6.168664	100.9195	0.066272	0.050573	0.162572	0.041044	0.387448	2.061385	0.285752

Determinant resid covariance (dof adj.)	1.06E-07
Determinant resid covariance	5.09E-09
Log likelihood	-2236.396
Akaike information criterion	17.42762
Schwarz criterion	27.80342

Bei Fragen zur Produktsicherheit wenden Sie sich bitte an:
If you have any questions regarding product safety,
please contact:

Walter de Gruyter GmbH
Genthiner Straße 13
10785 Berlin
productsafety@degruyterbrill.com